"Global Doodle Gems" Flower Collection Volume 1

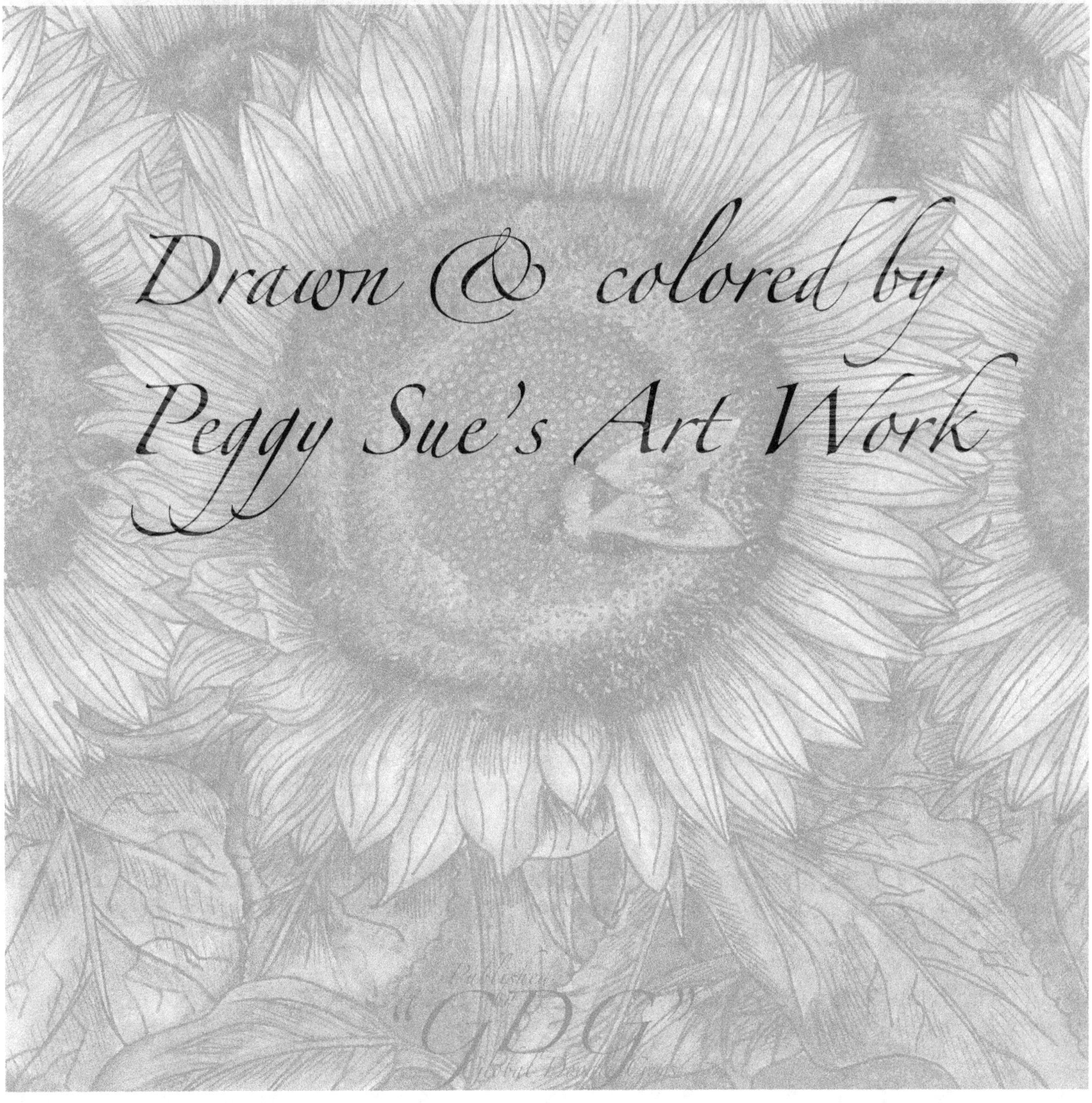

Drawn & colored by Peggy Sue's Art Work

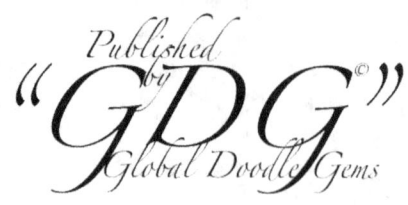

Share your colored versions with us ! We love seeing your results and hearing from you we are social !

The Official FB book page, stay on top of what we have in the works !
www.facebook.com/globaldoodlegems

The Community group, share your colored pages, meet the artists, enjoy exclusive freebies, take part in community Charity books and so much more......
www.facebook.com/groups/globaldoodlegems/

Follow us on Twitter.... @GlobalDoodlegem

We are on Instagram too
@globaldoodlegems for instagram

...and if you are not social like that we have a blog
globaldoodlegems.wordpress.com

Copyright © 2015 Global Doodle Gems

All rights are reserved by Global Doodle Gems.

Duplication of pages for personal use are allowed. You are invited to color the pages then scan/post your coloured versions to social networks, mentioning the book title and author/artist (Global Doodle Gems).

All artwork and images are protected by copyright laws. This book or any portion thereof may not, otherwise, be reproduced and/or distributed or transmitted without the express written permission of the artist/publisher of Global Doodle Gems.

All of us from the Global Doodle Gems wish you a colortastic time and look forward to seeing your wonderful color results online !

Participating Artists

1. Bev Choy
2. DomDomx
3. Pica Wu
4. Joseph Shivery
5. Jane Levi
6. Yaya
7. Marieke Raterman-Bos
8. Lynne McGee
9. Peggy Sue's ArtWork
10. T.J.
11. Iben Lykke Højholdt
12. Gloria Lenzen
13. Maud Feral Chauveau (MFC)
14. Audrey Sagh
15. Nicole Whelan

Contributing Artist
Bev Choy
USA

Facebook : bevchoyart
Facebook Group : MixedMediaSupport
Etsy : BevChoyArt

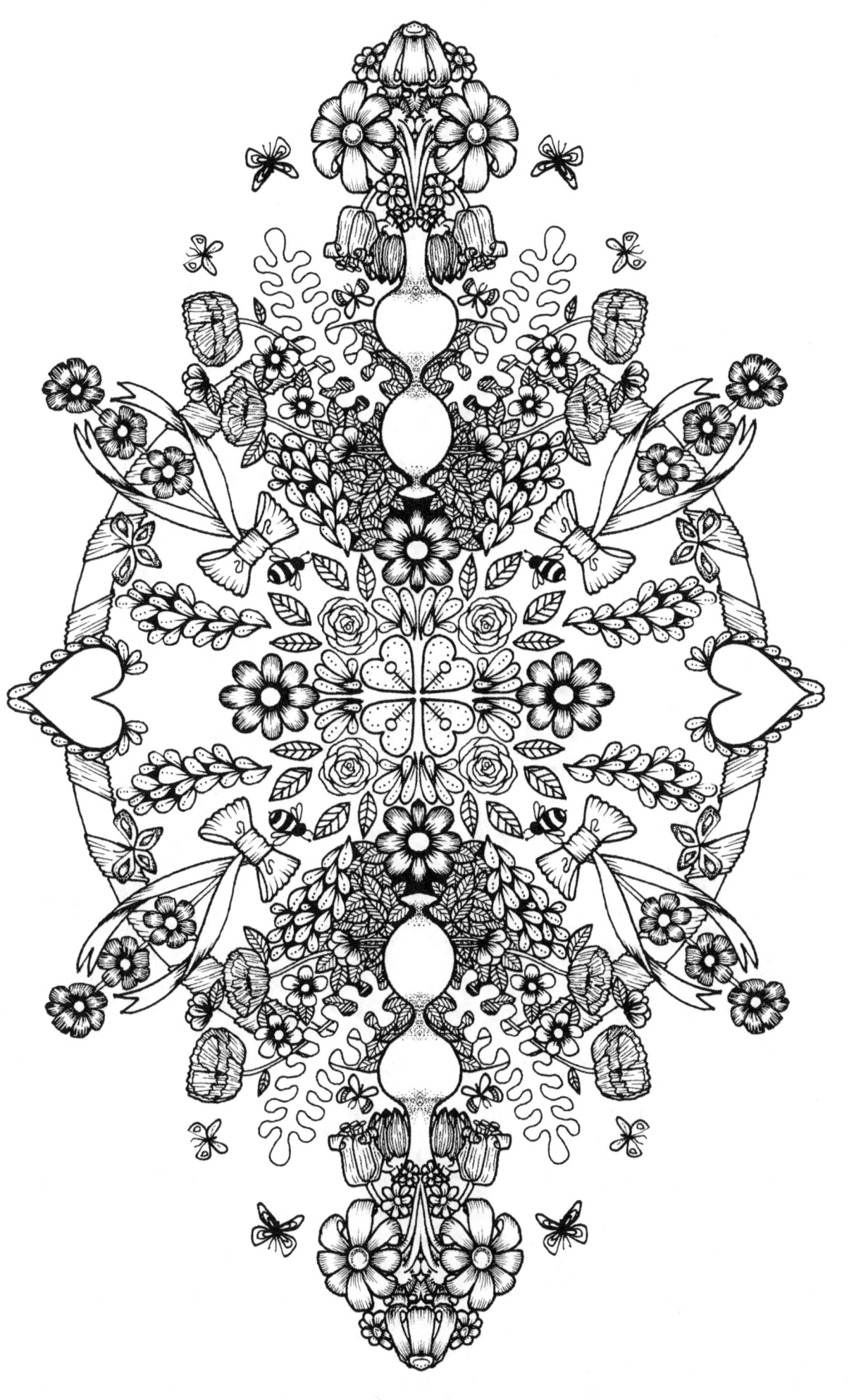

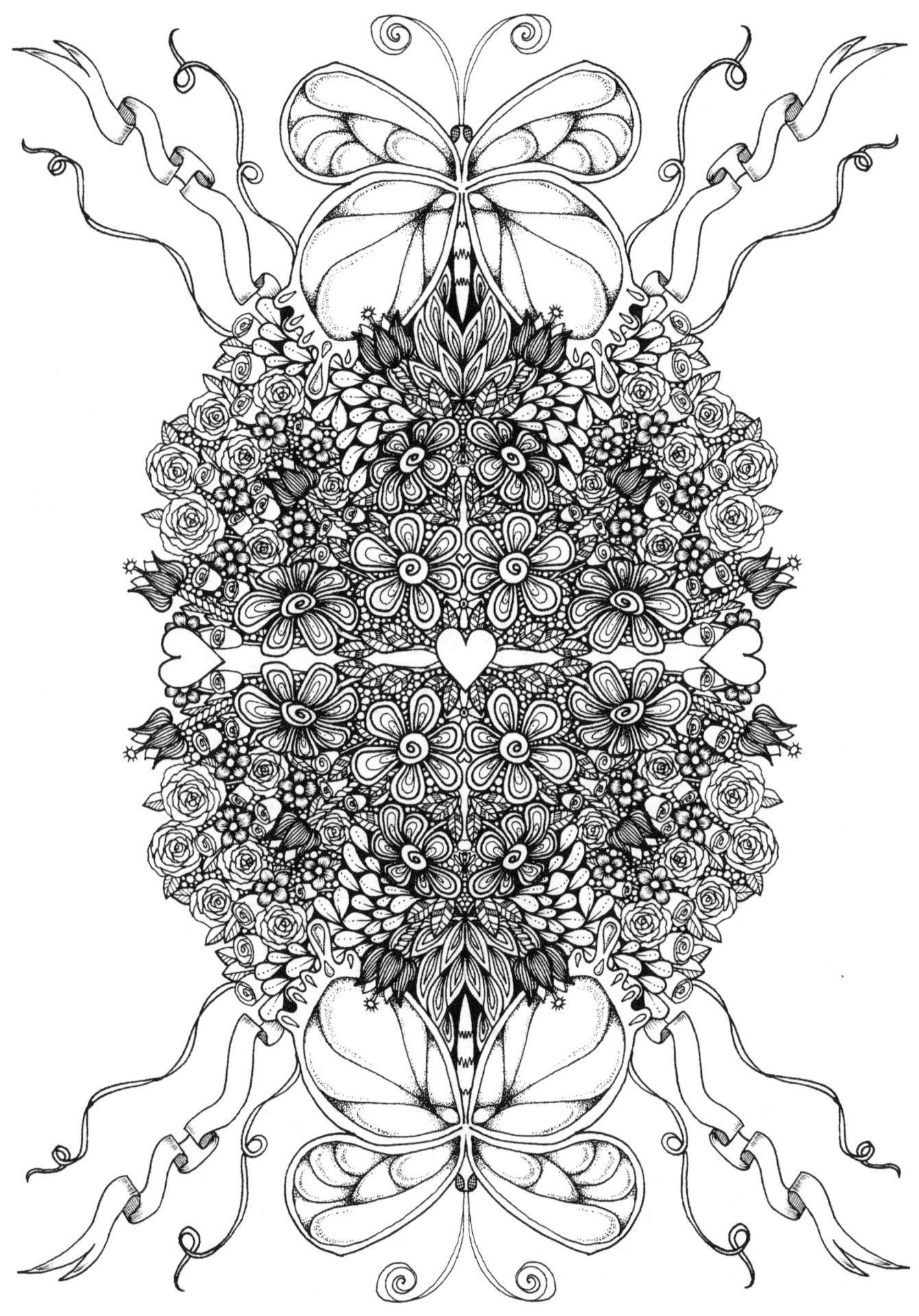

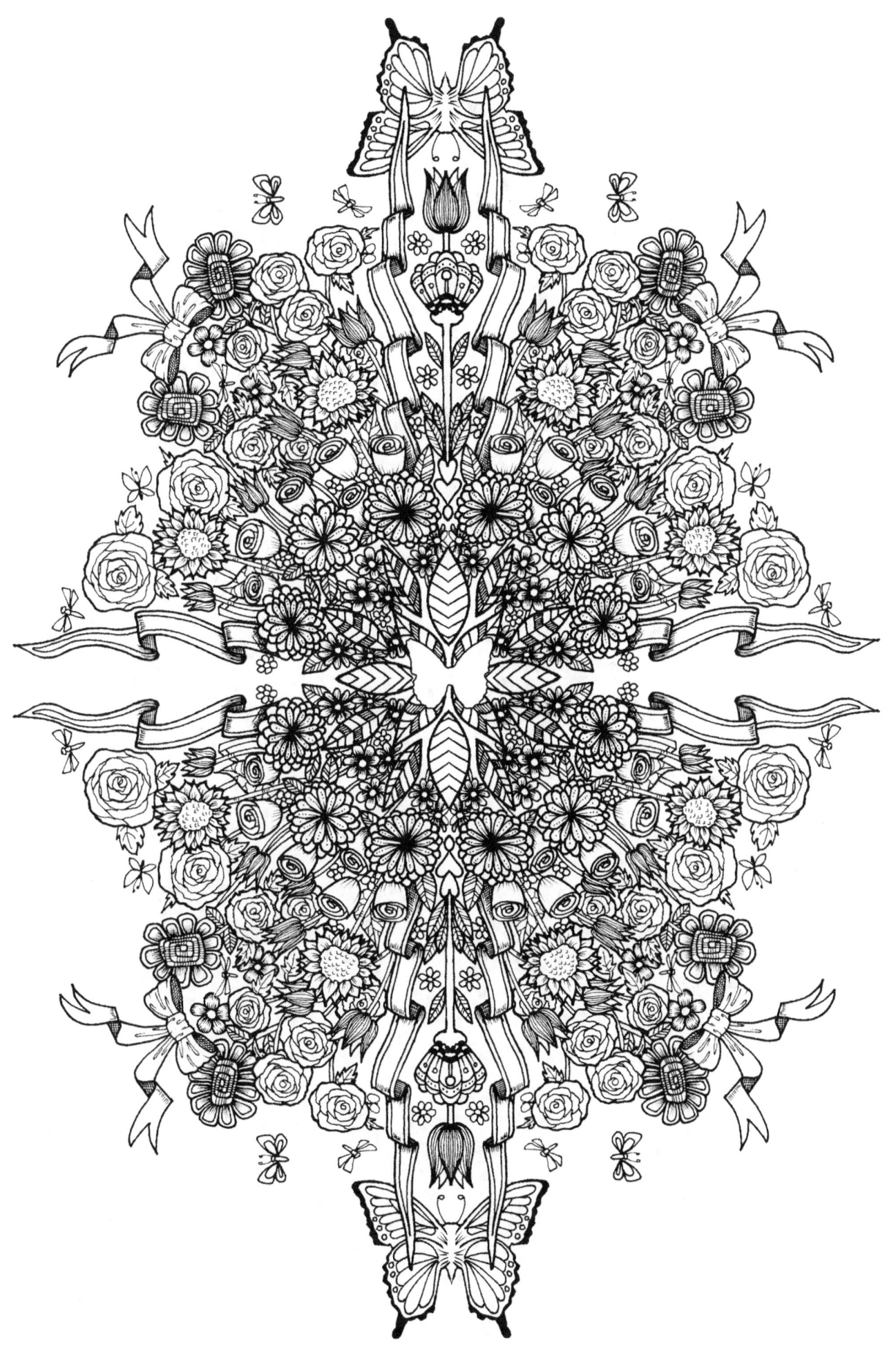

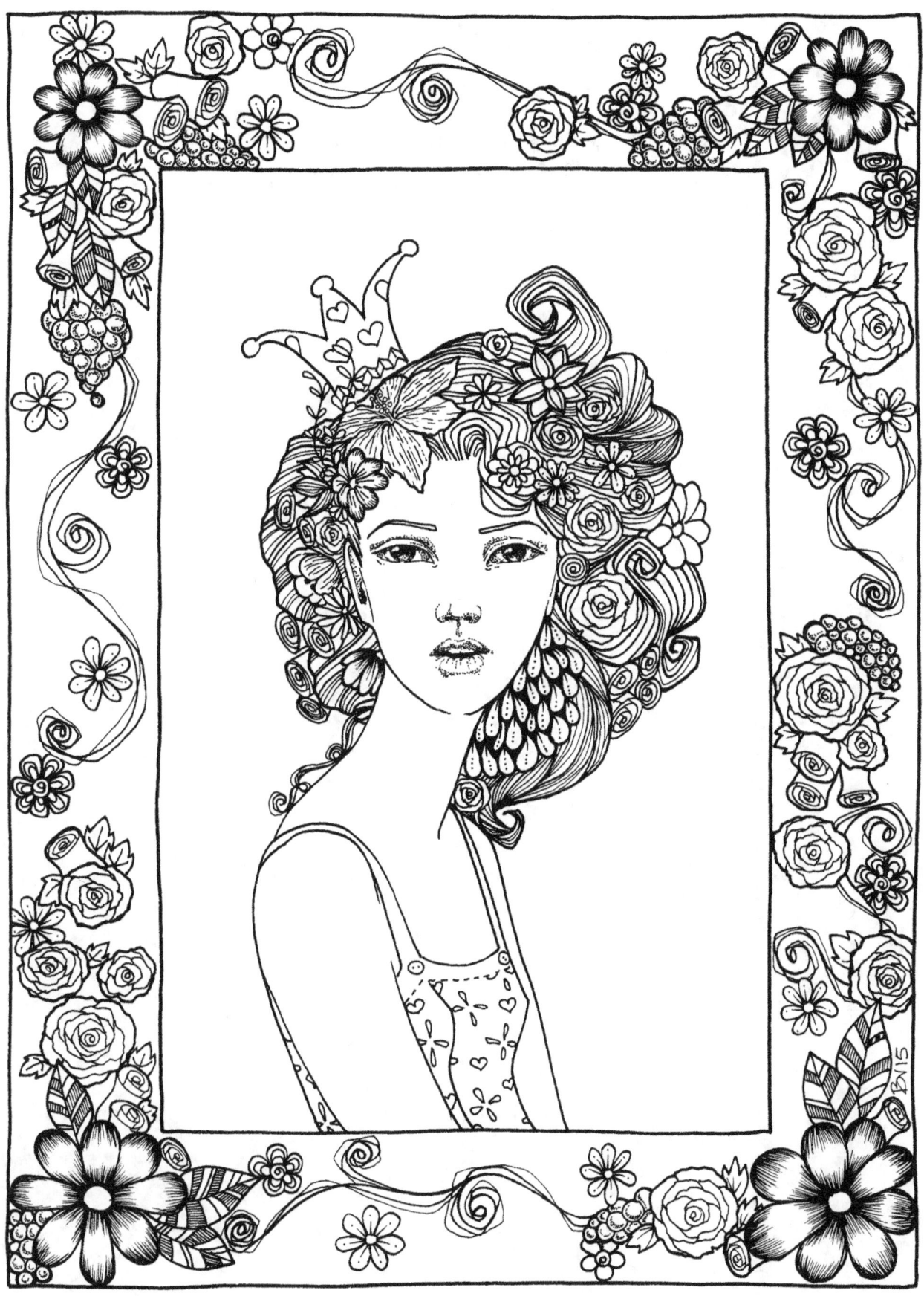

Contributing Artist
DomDomx
France

Facebook : Les-dessins-et-doodles-de-Dom-Domx
Facebook Group : Color.Addict

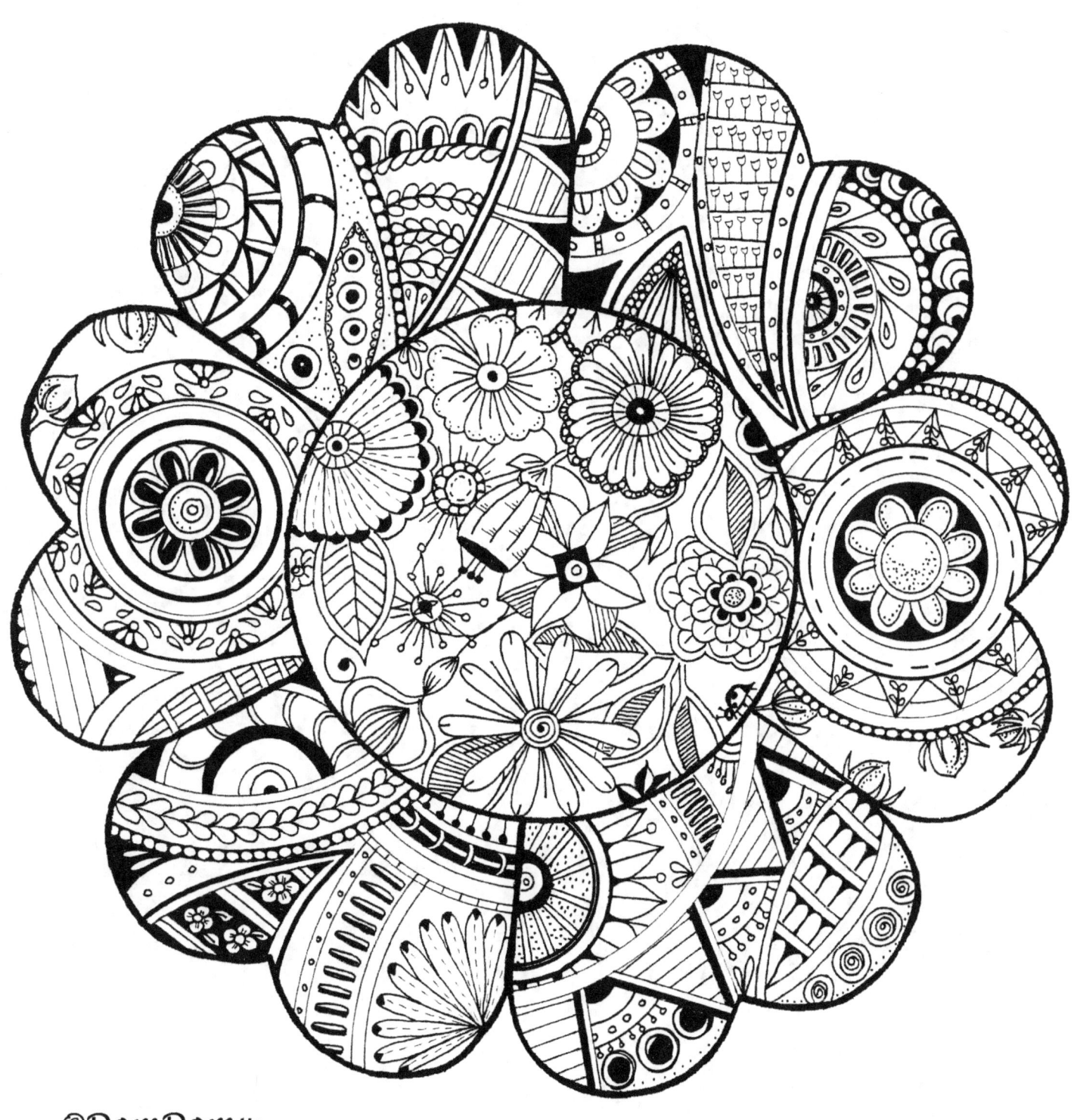

DomDomx

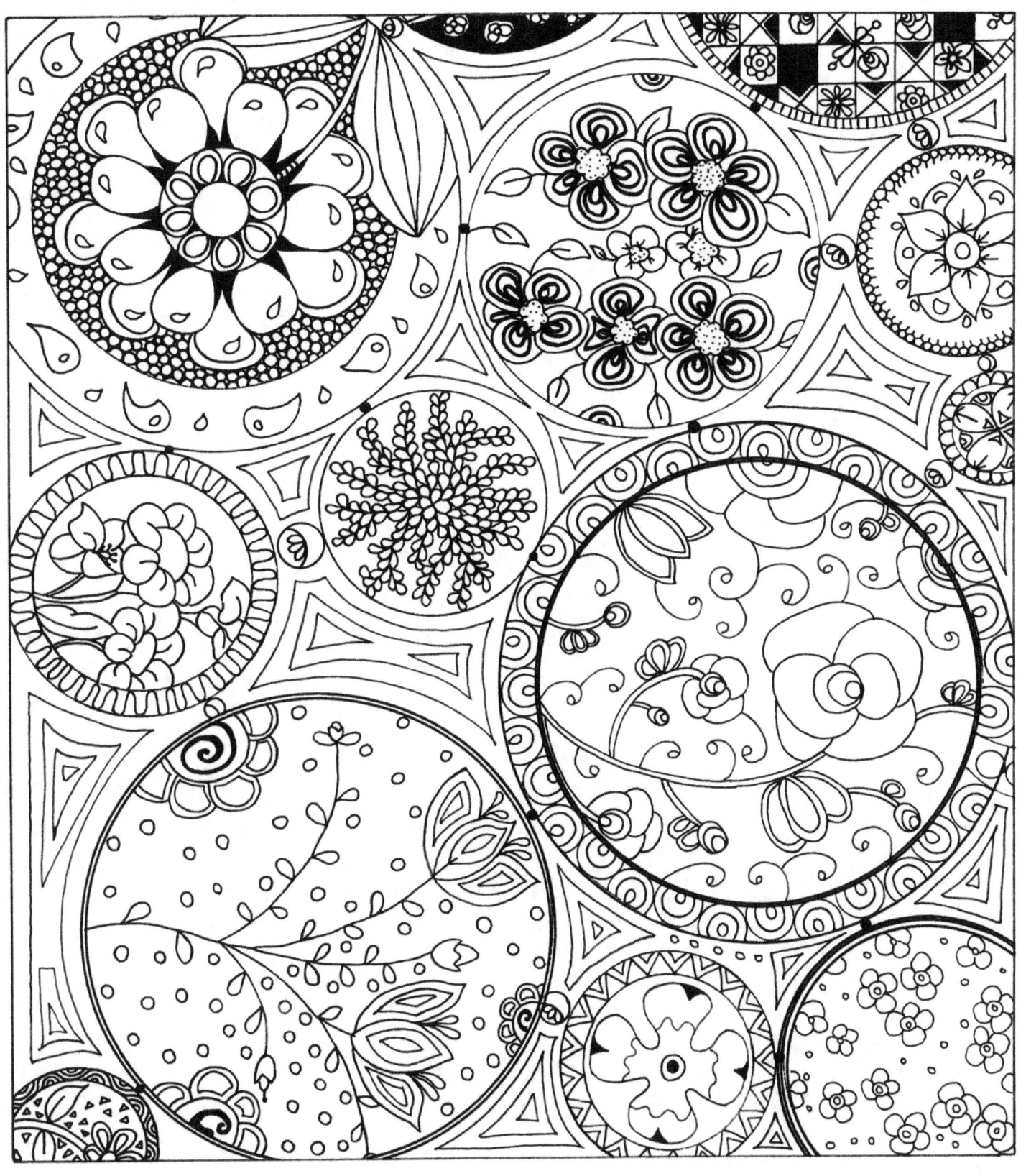

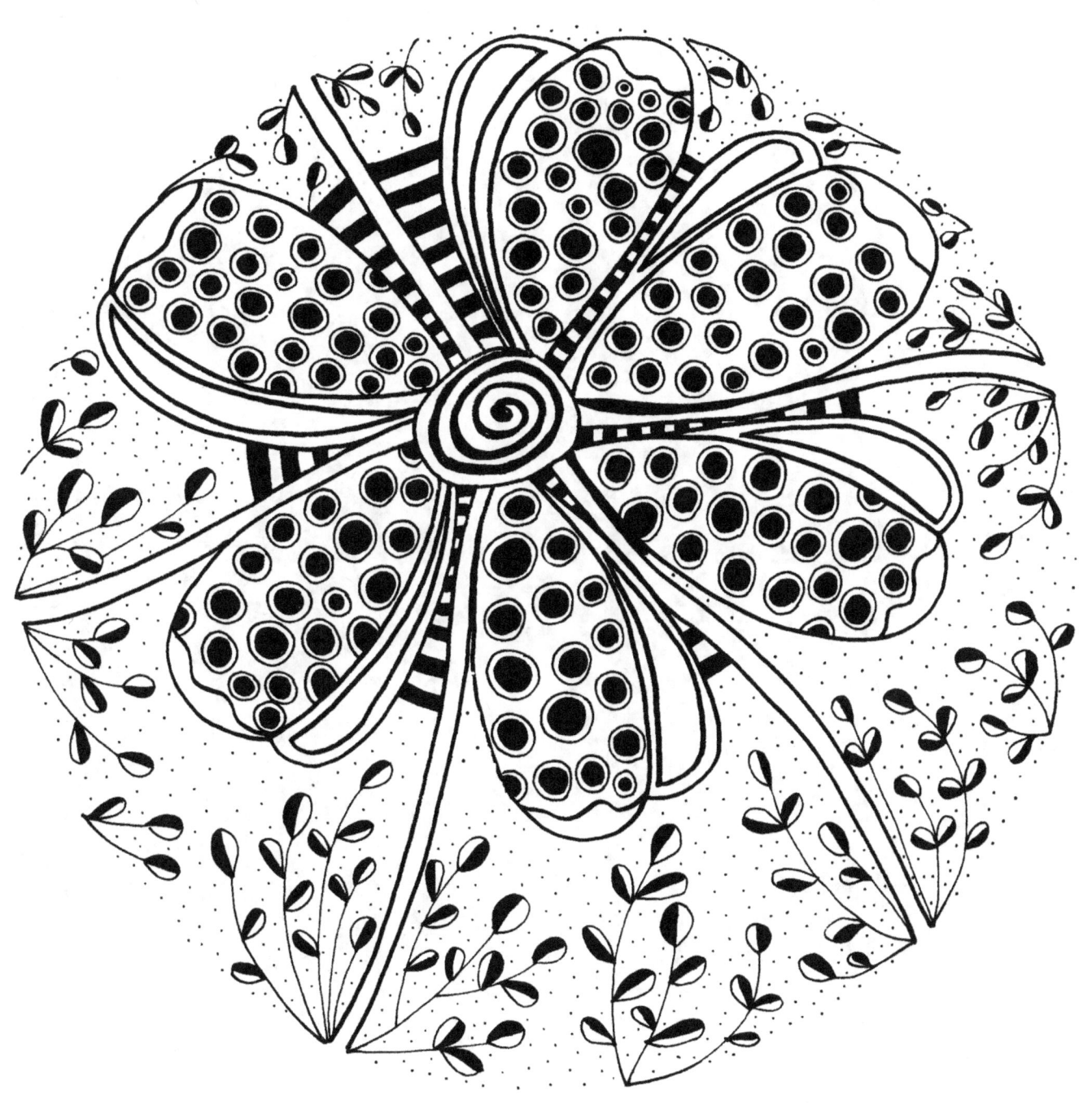

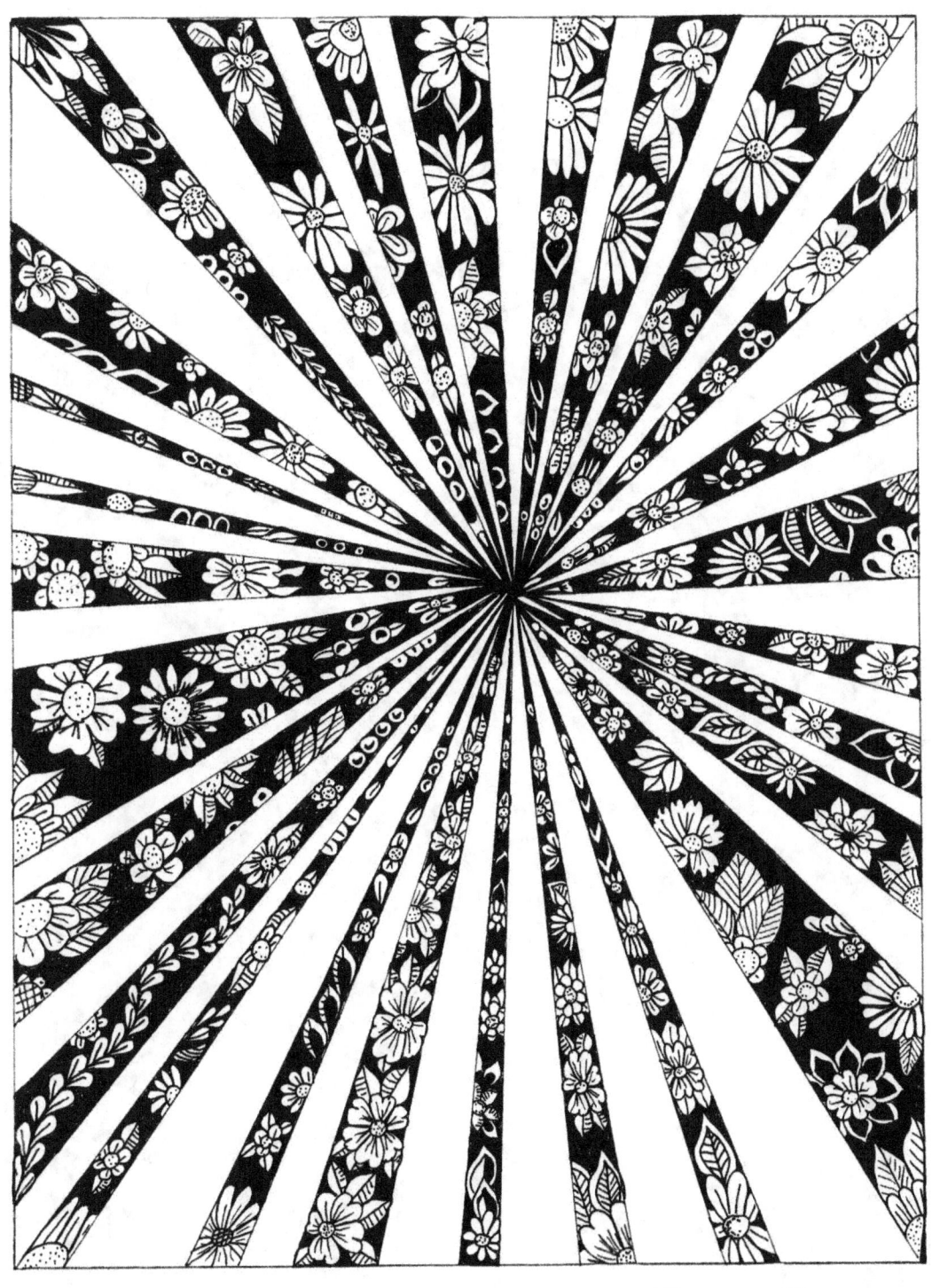

Contributing Artist
Pica Wu
Taiwan

Facebook : picapicadrow2

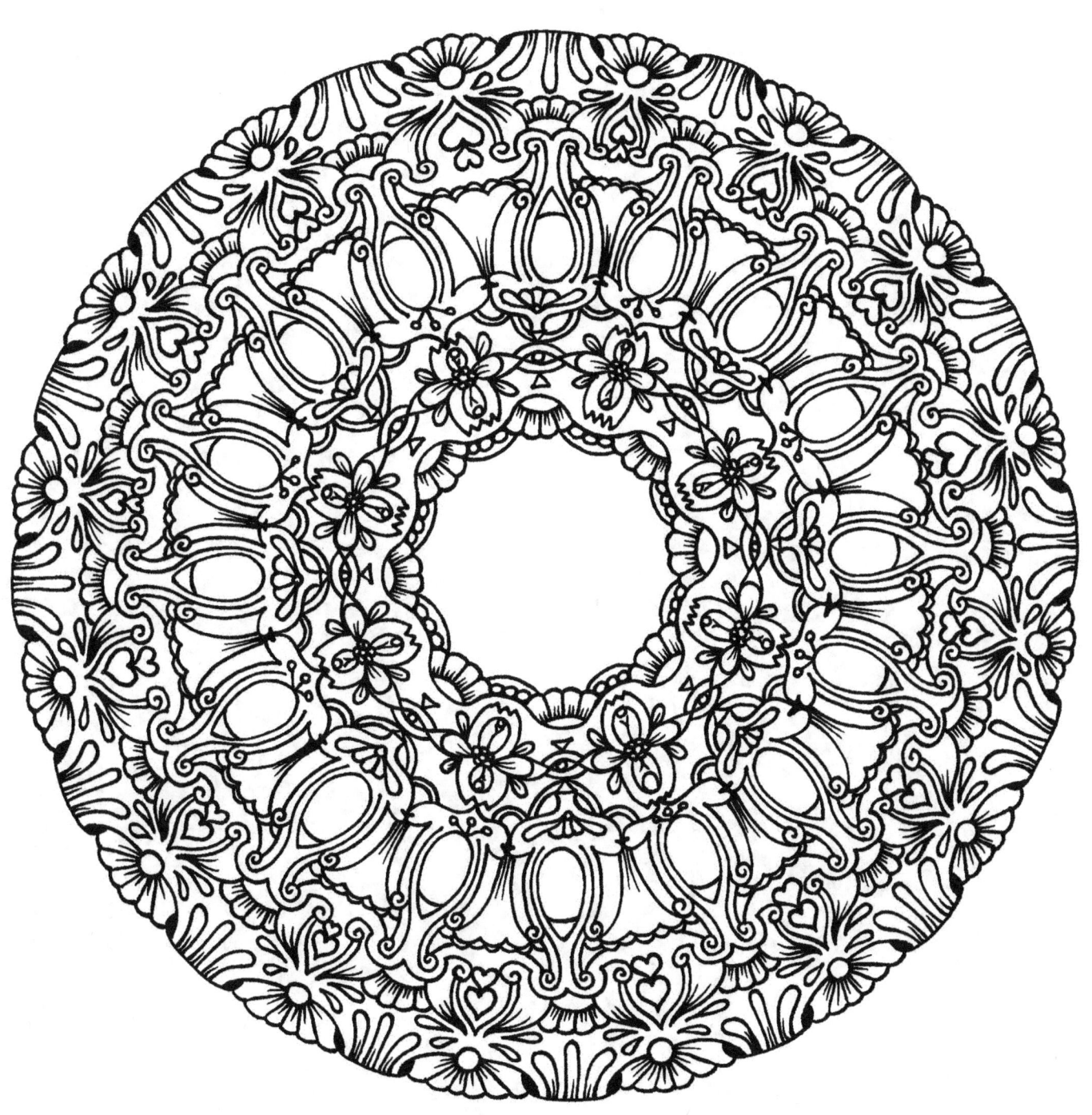

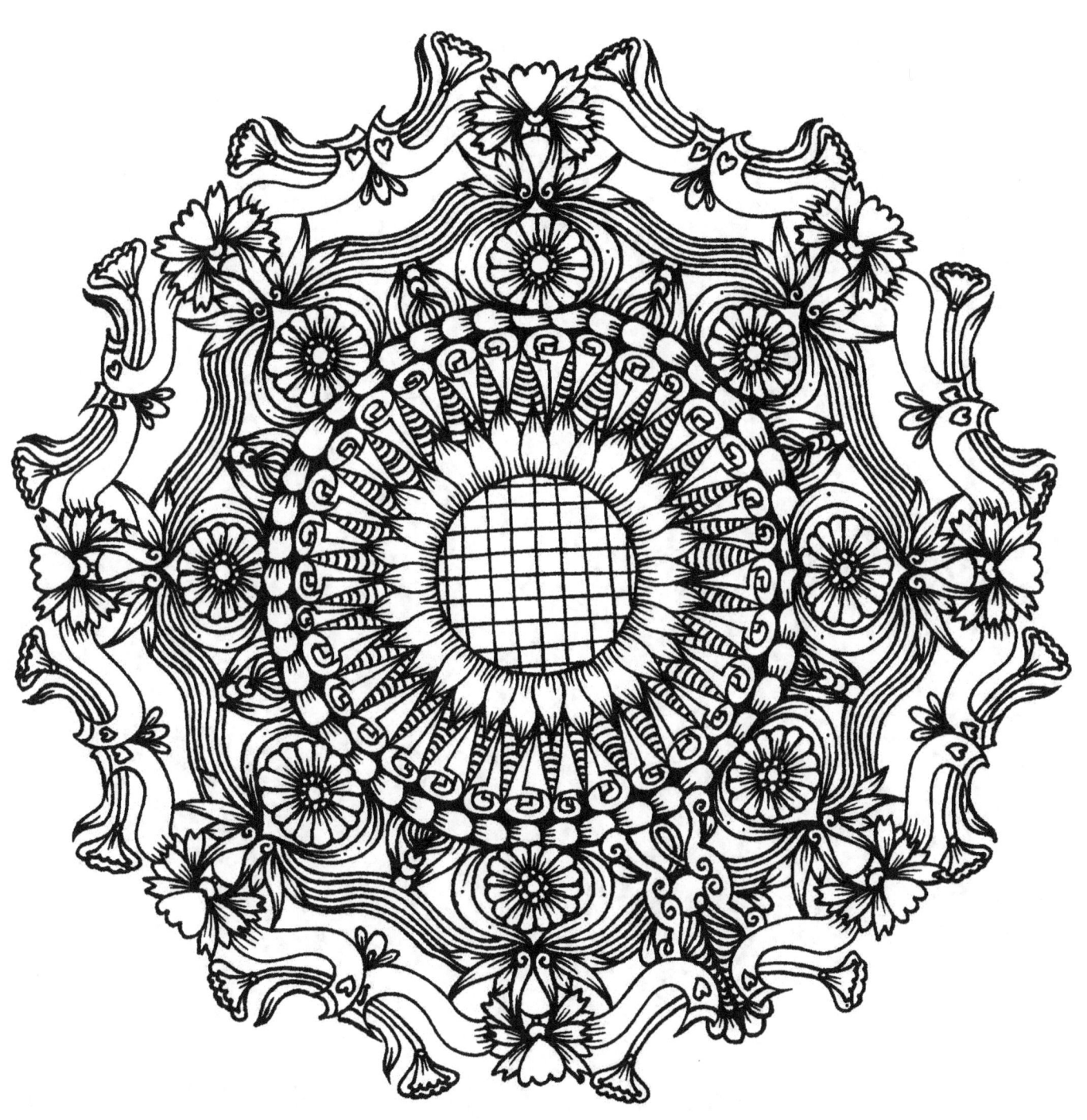

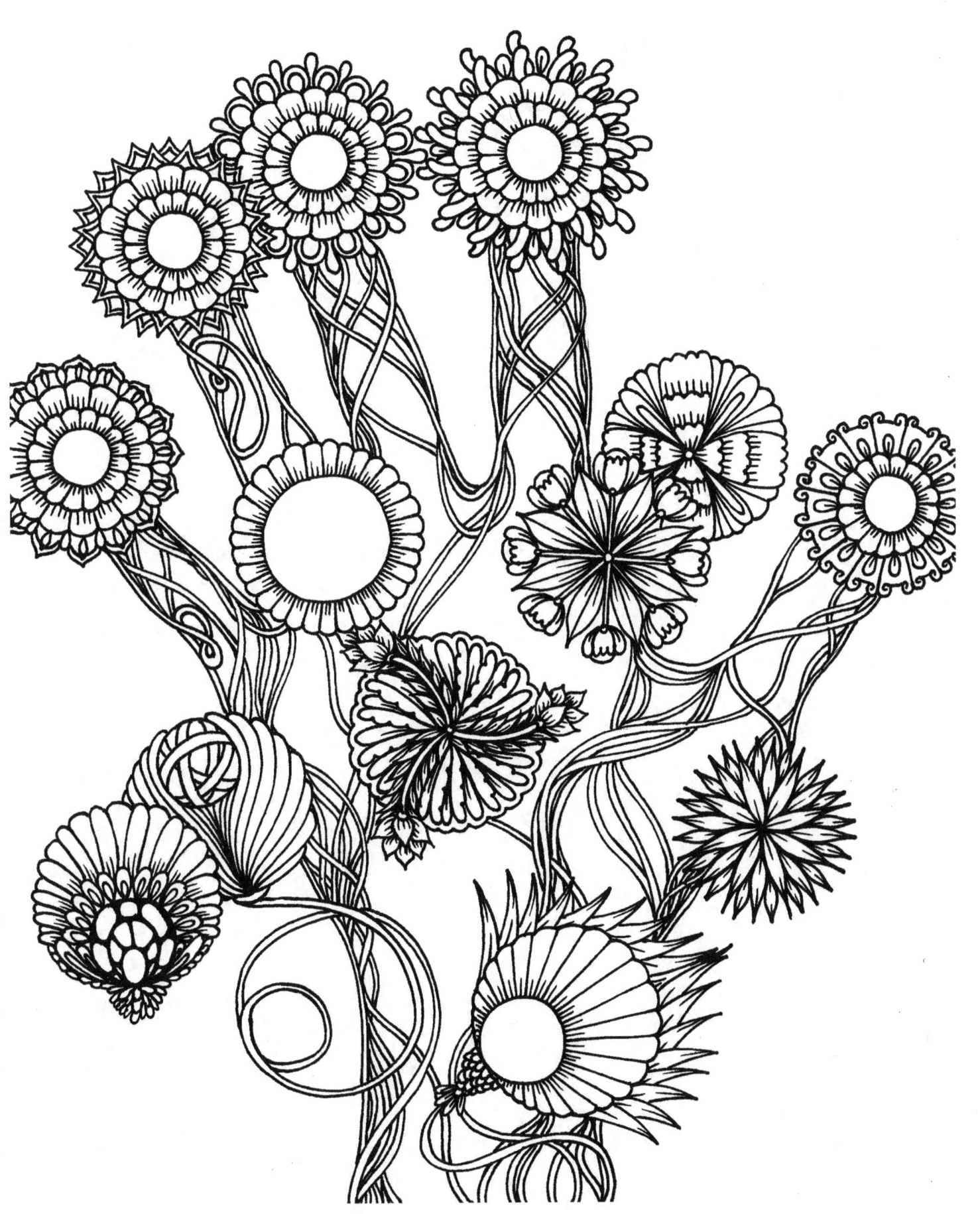

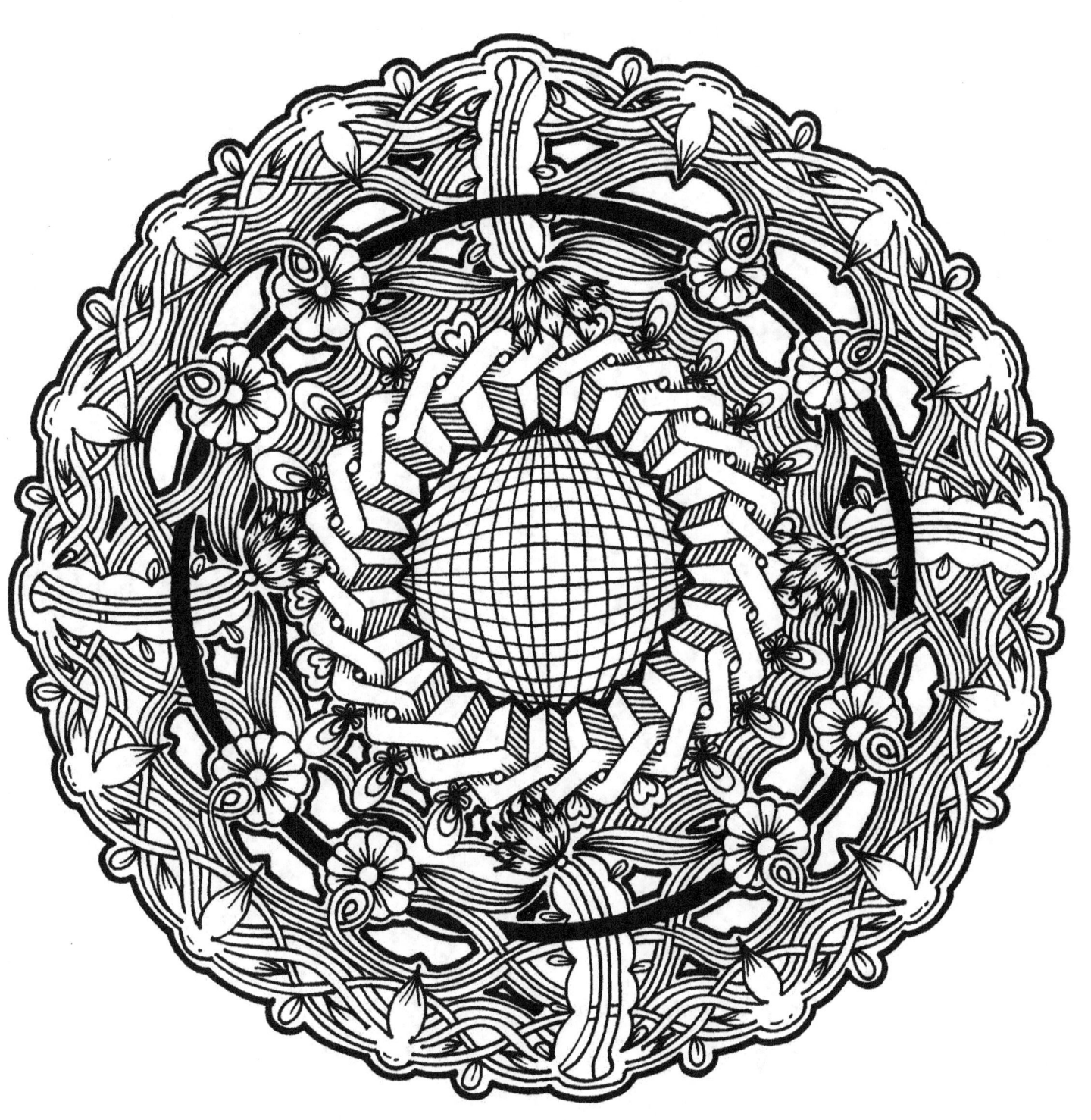

Contributing Artist
Joseph Shivery
USA

Facebook : The-Broken-Mind-of-Joes-Ink
Payhip shop : joesinkearthlinknet

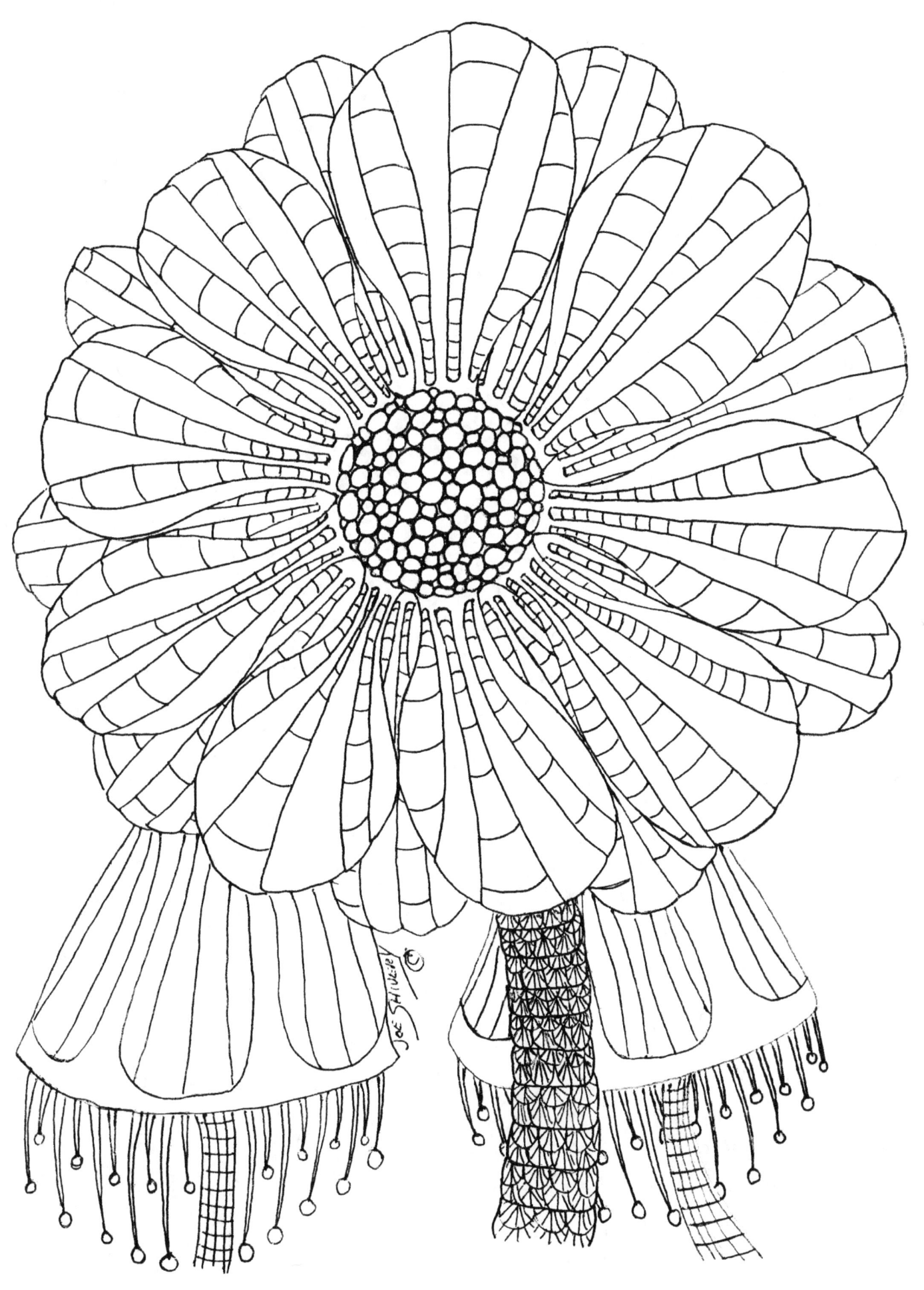

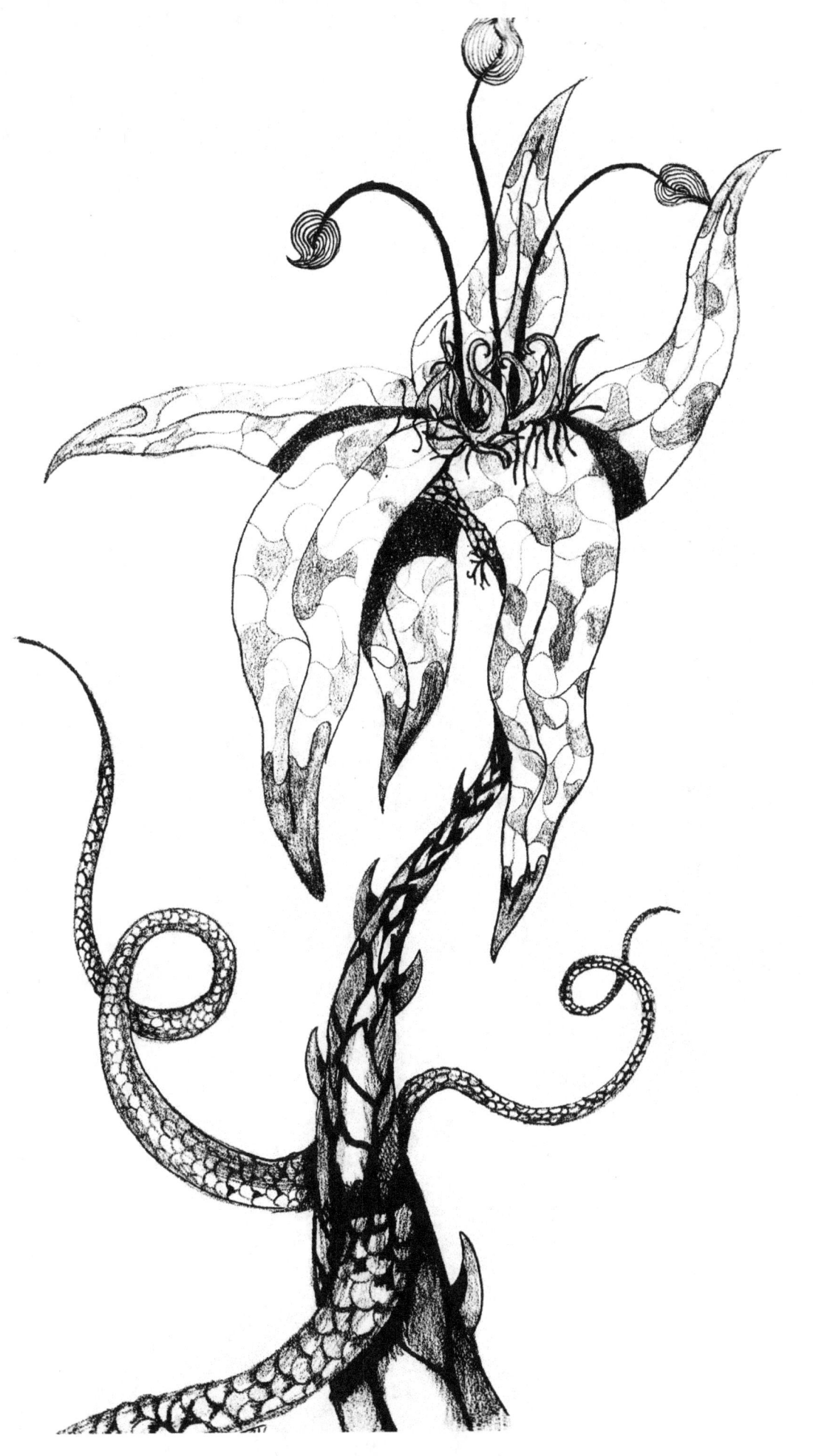

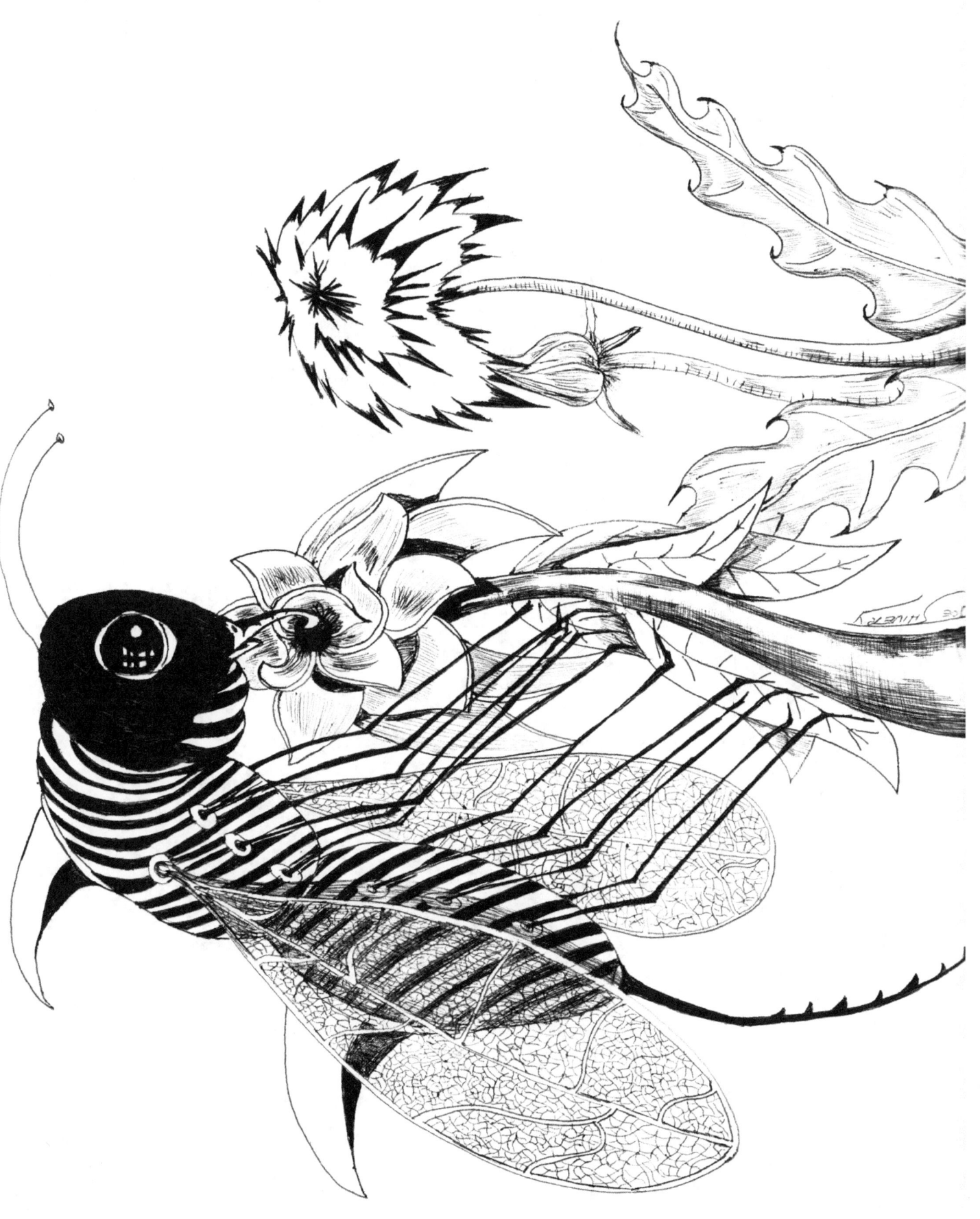

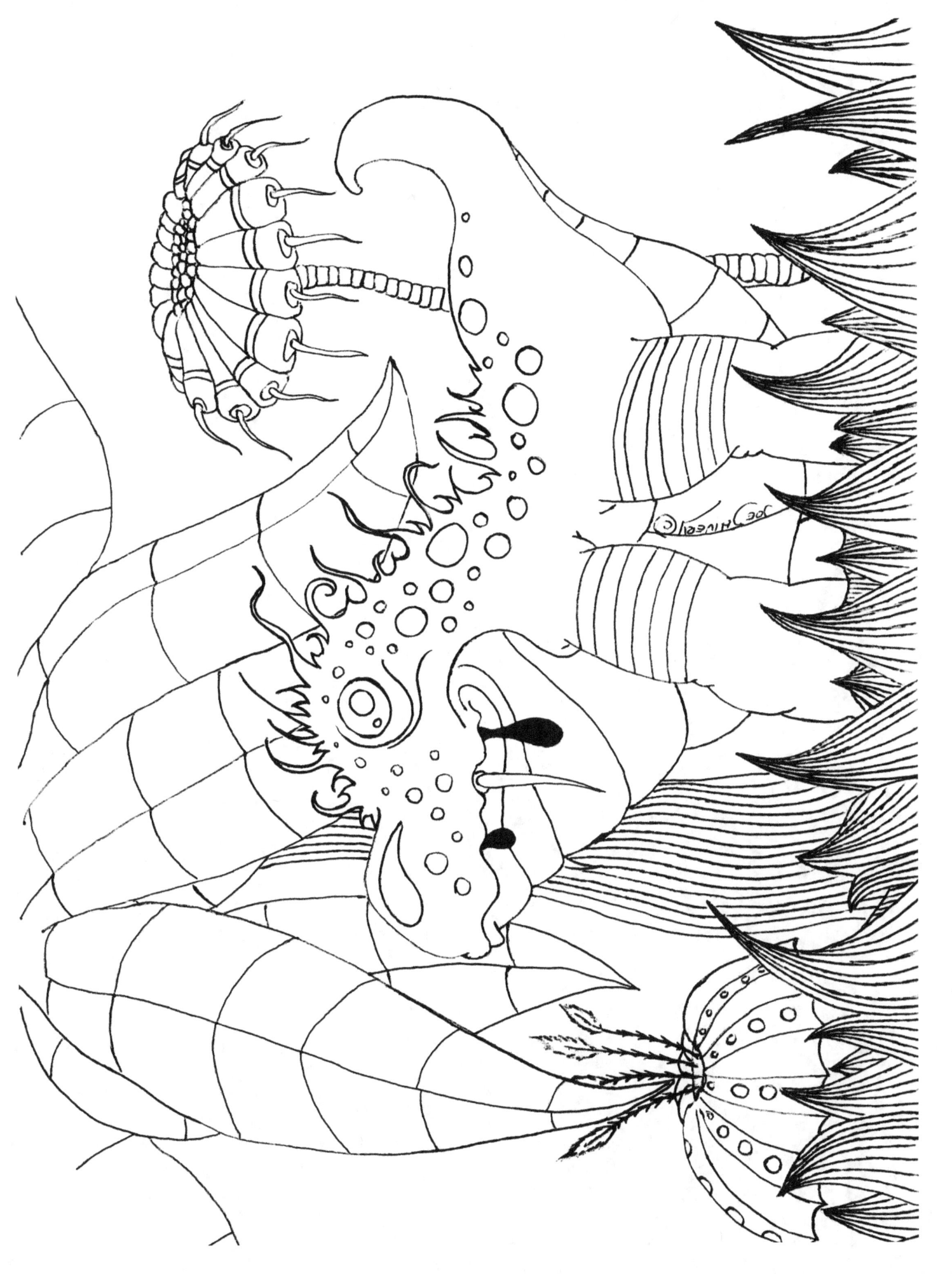

Contributing Artist
Jane Levi
France

Facebook : Cheeky-Cats

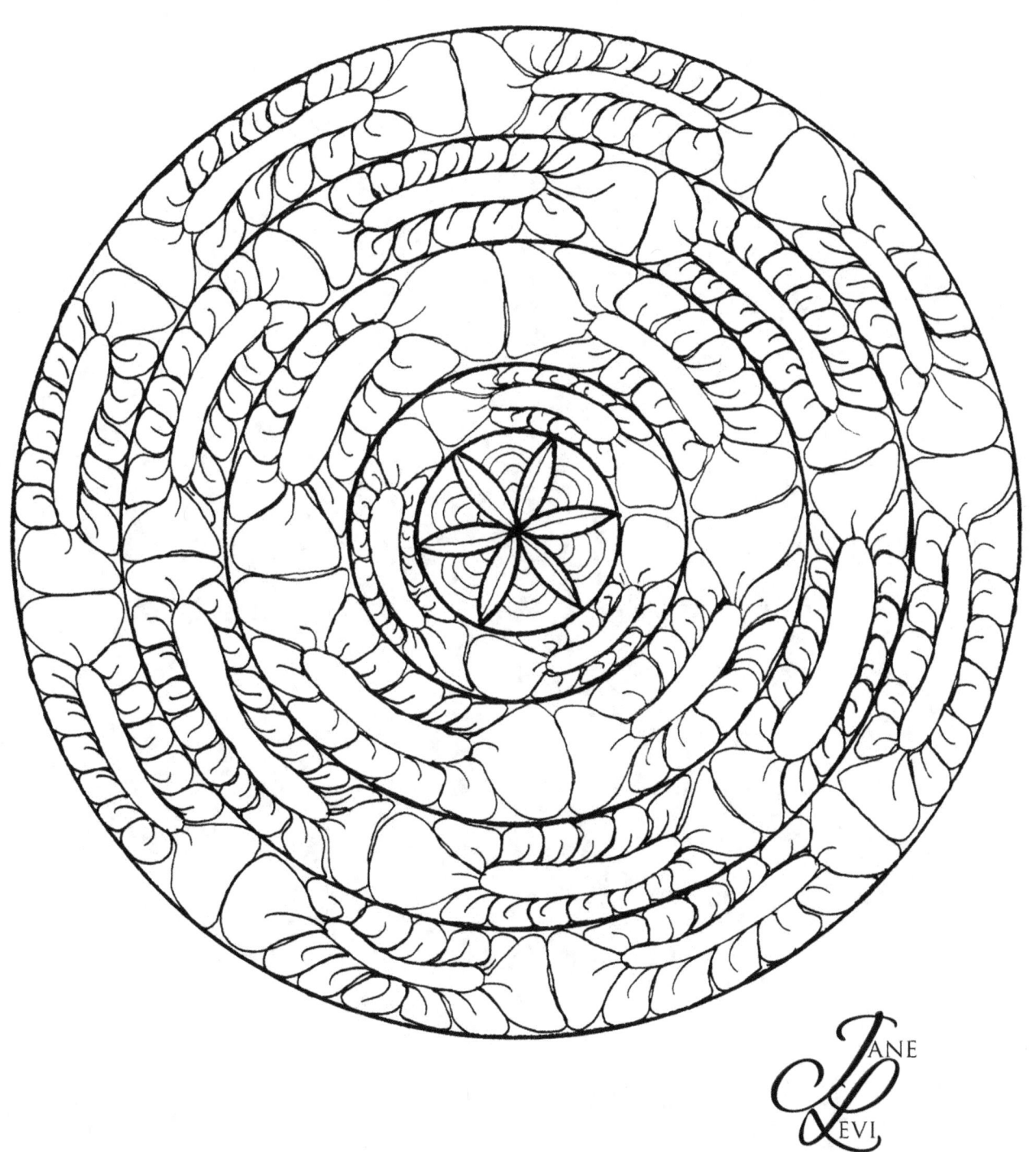

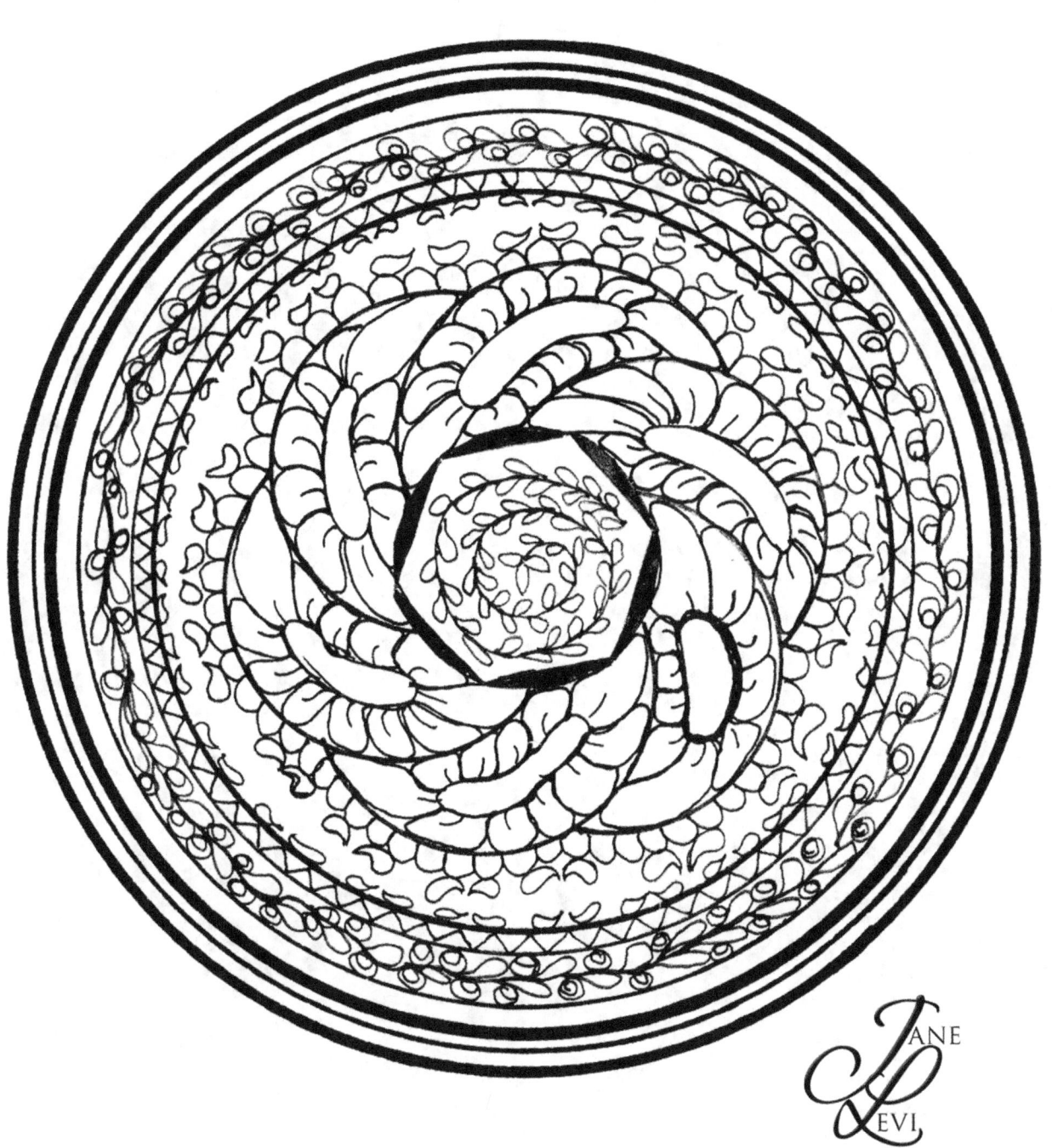

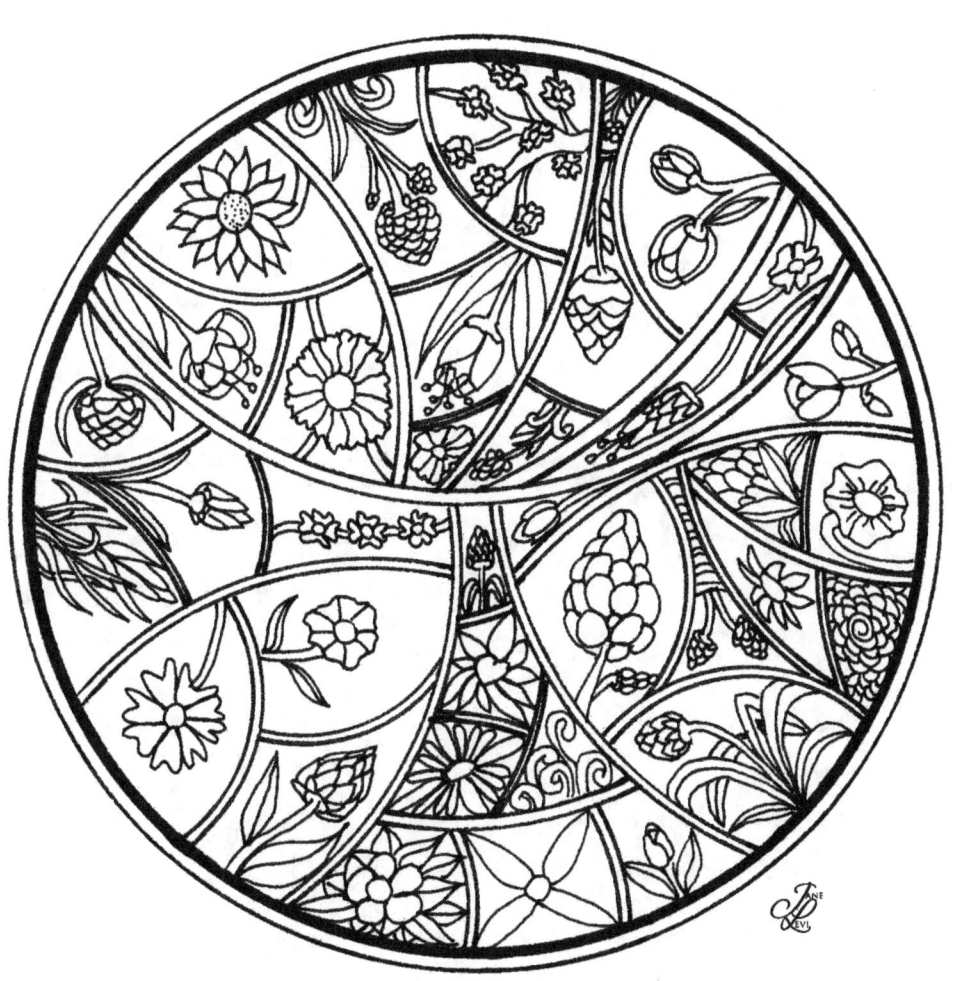

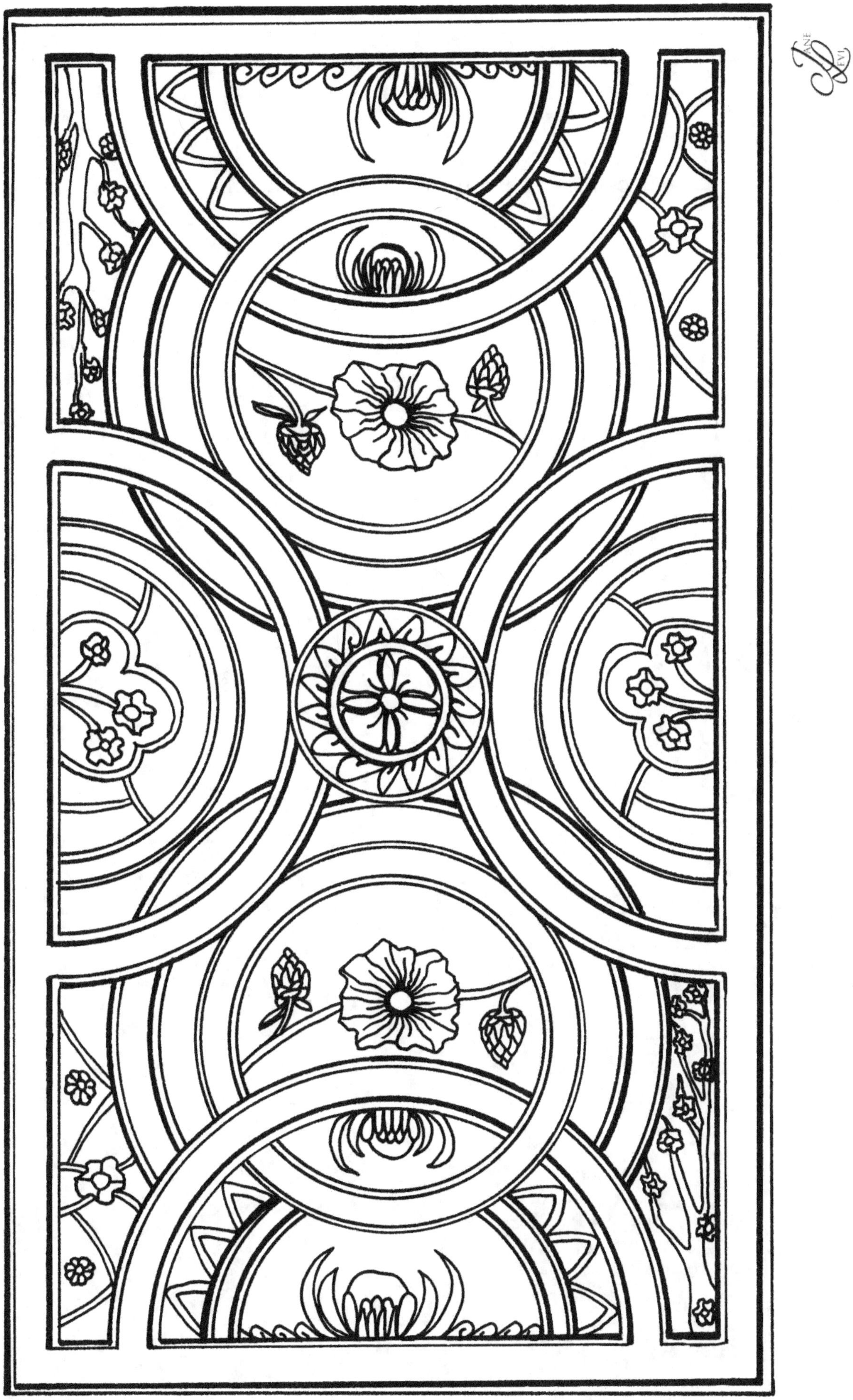

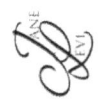

Contributing Artist
Yaya
France

Facebook : Les-gribouillis-de-yaya-georgia-merino

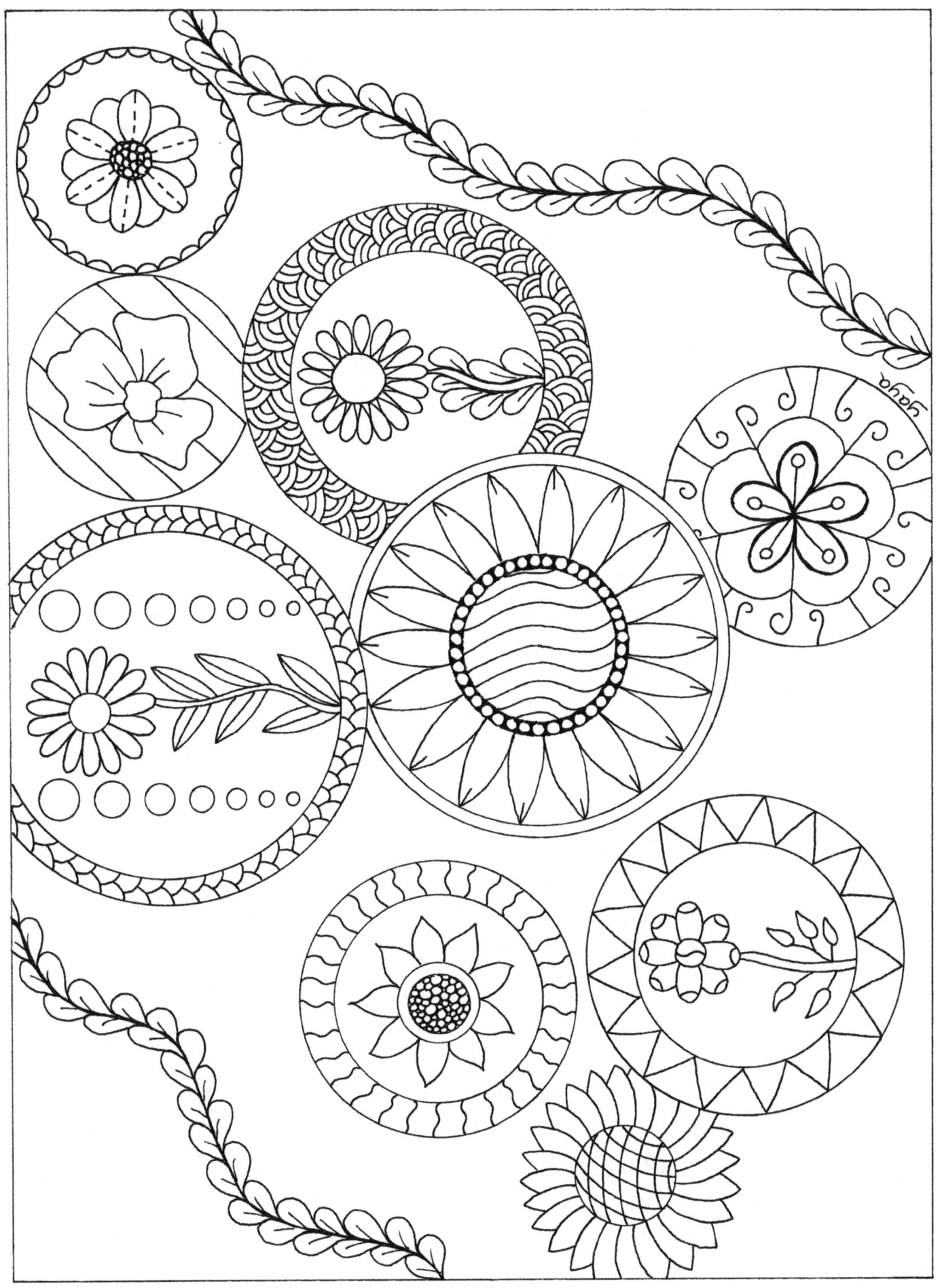

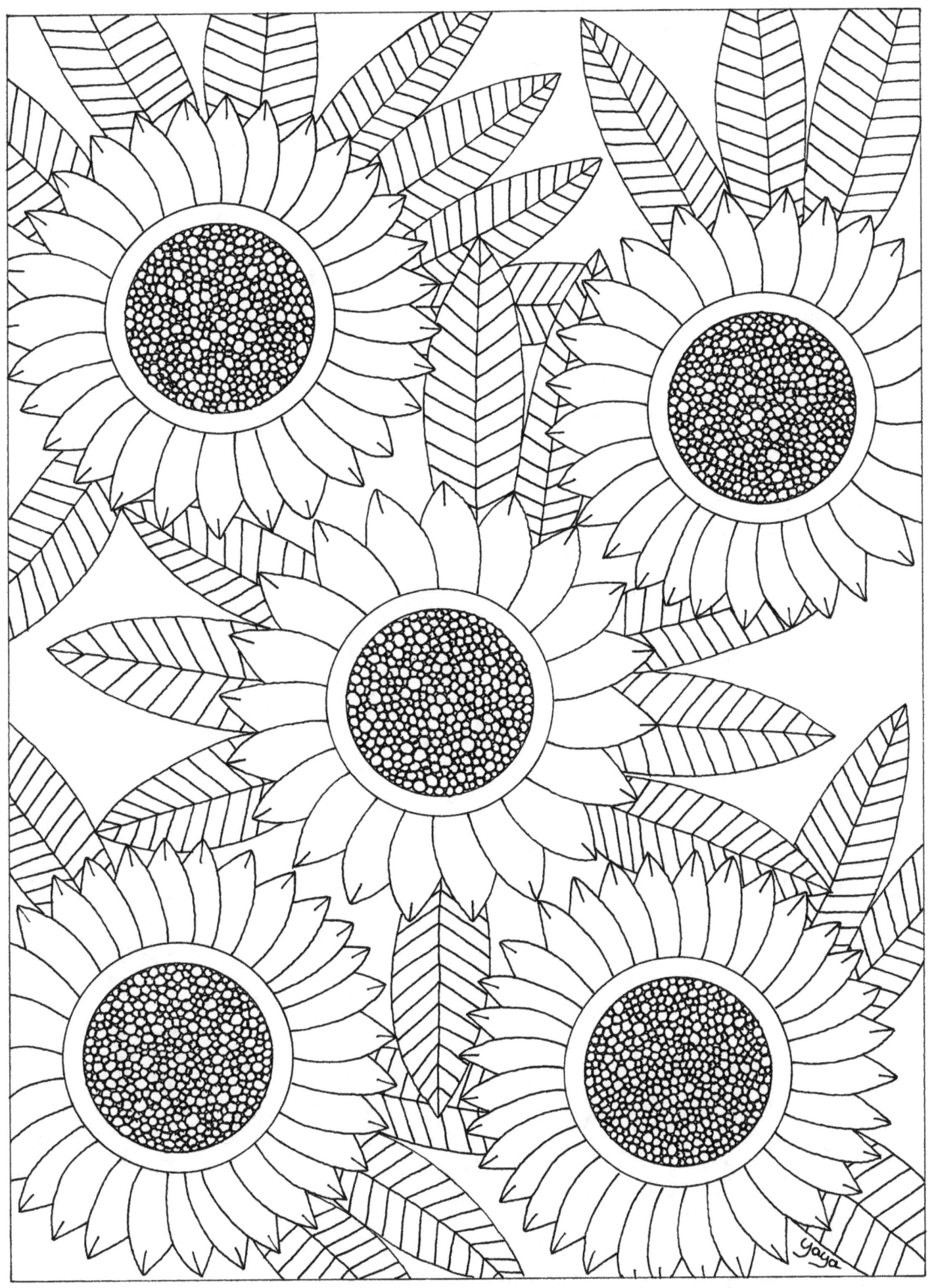

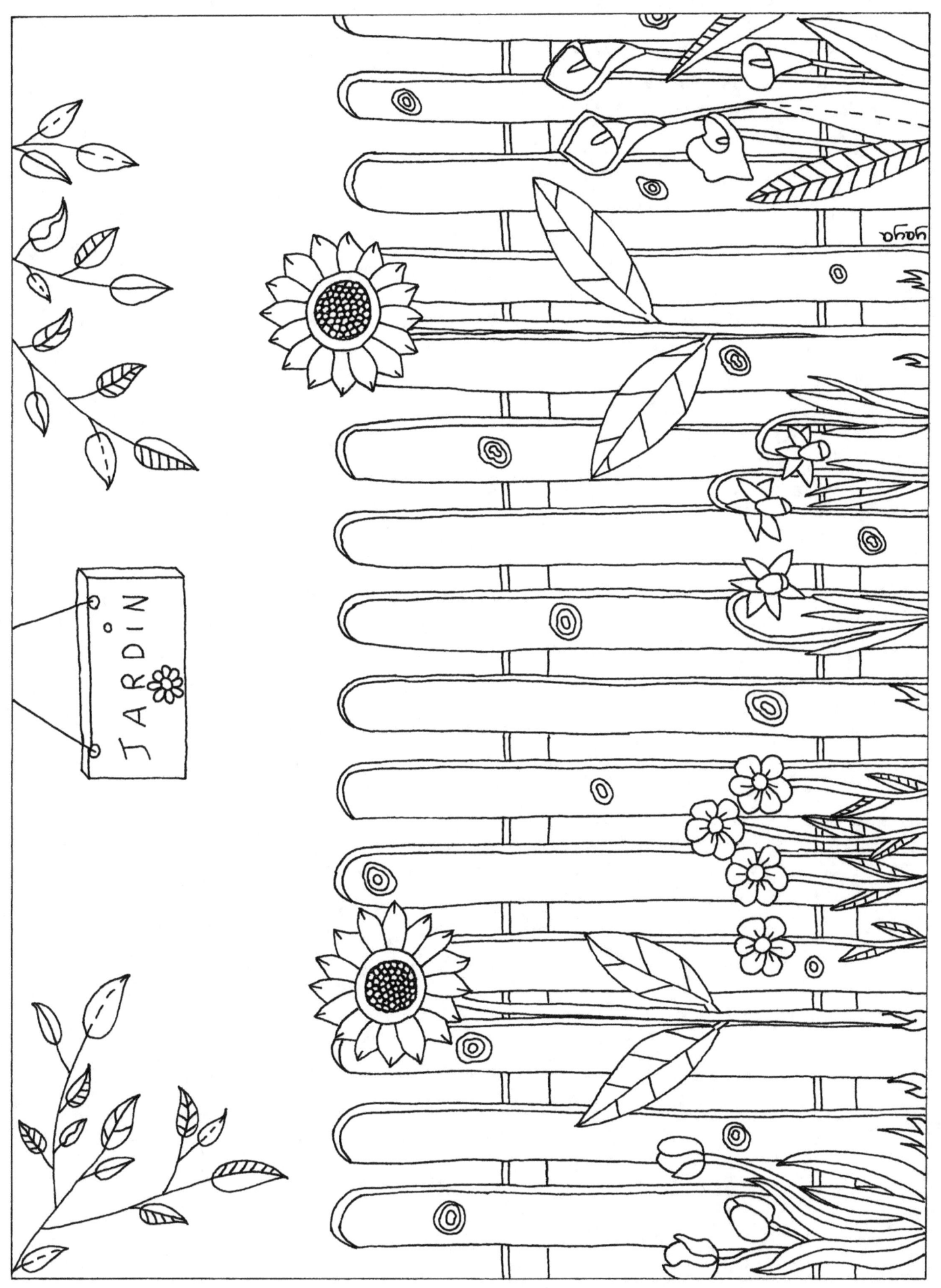

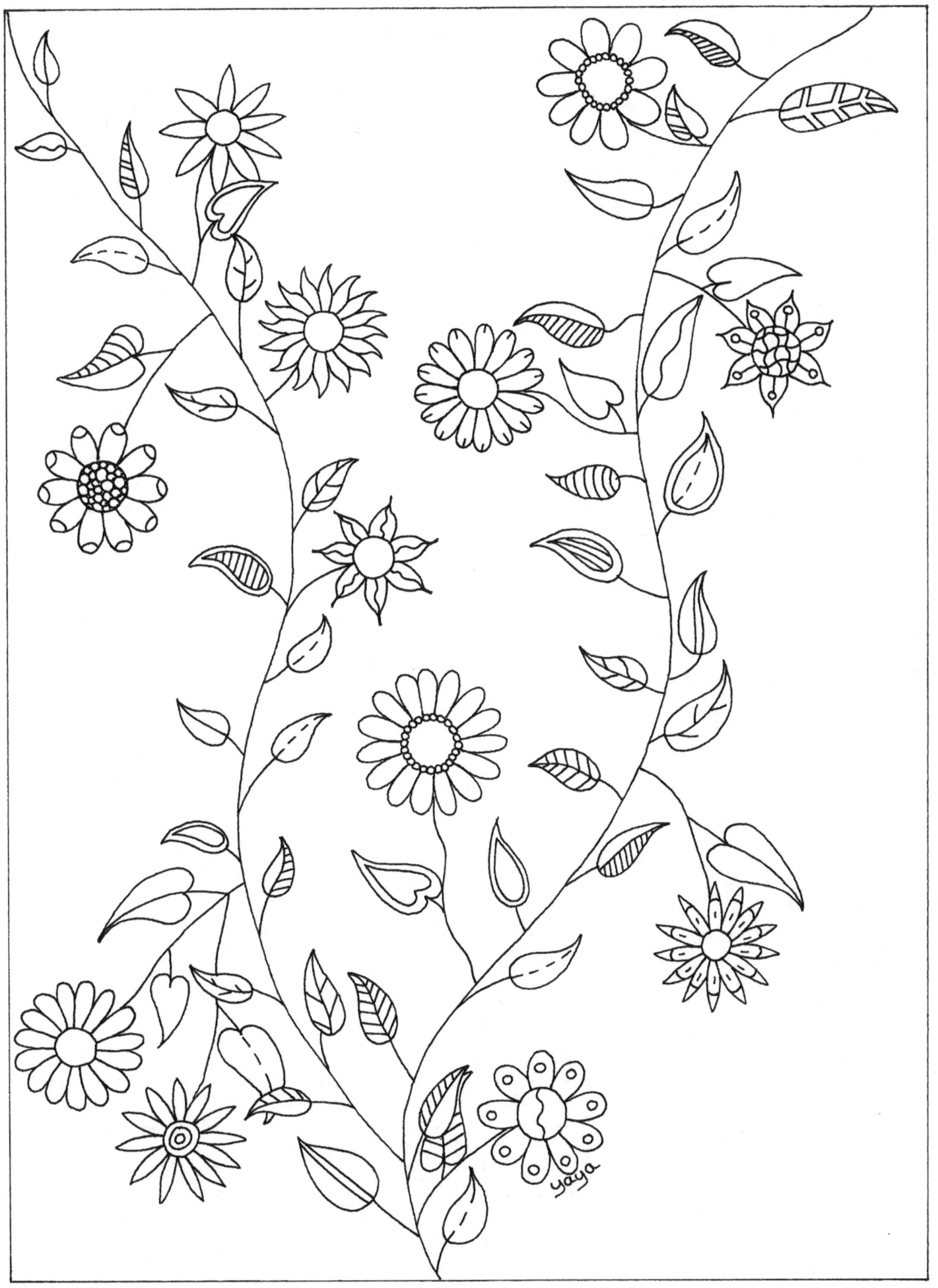

Contributing Artist
Marieke Raterman-Bos
Monnicken Werken
Monnickendam, the Netherlands

www.monnickenwerken.nl

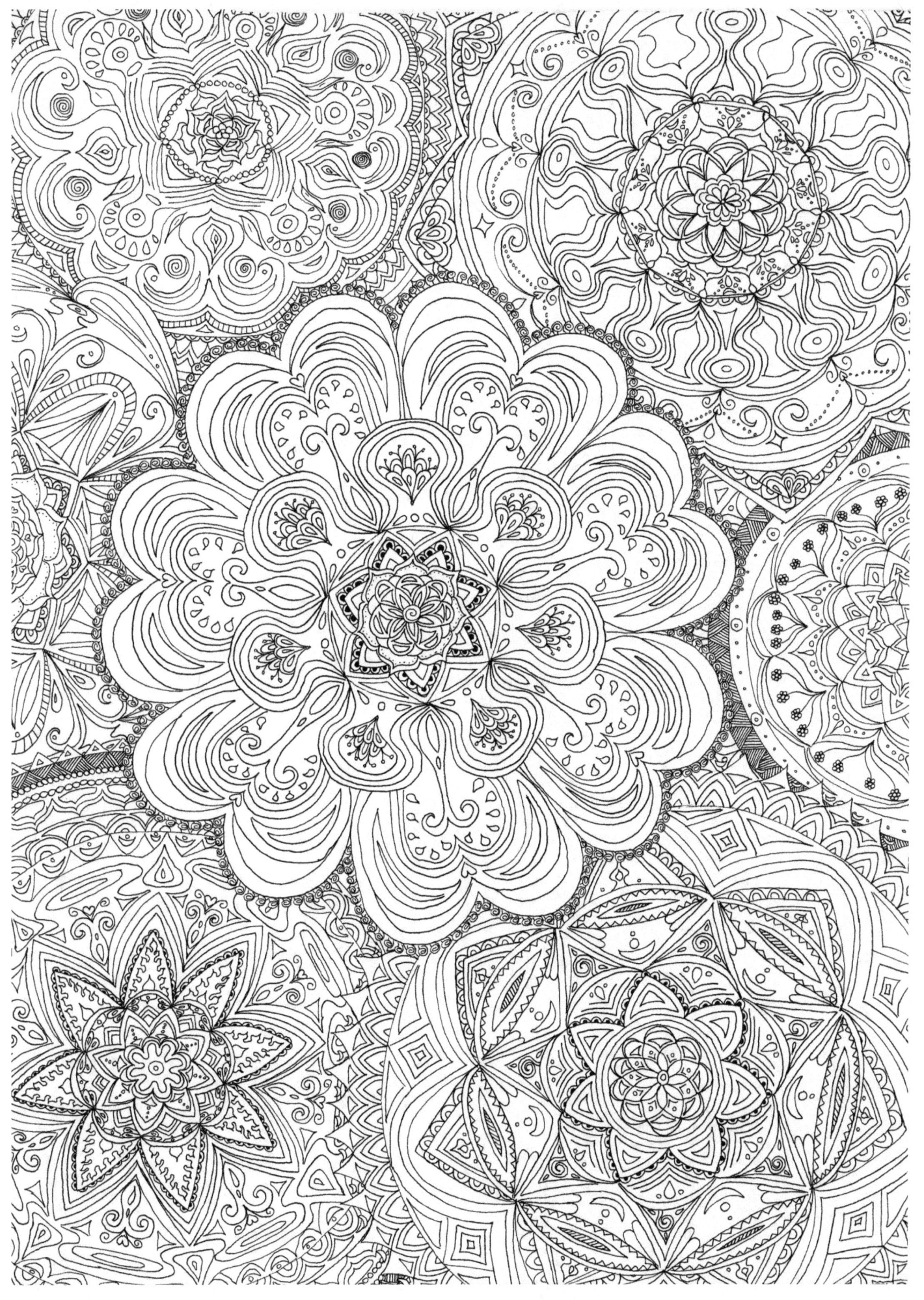

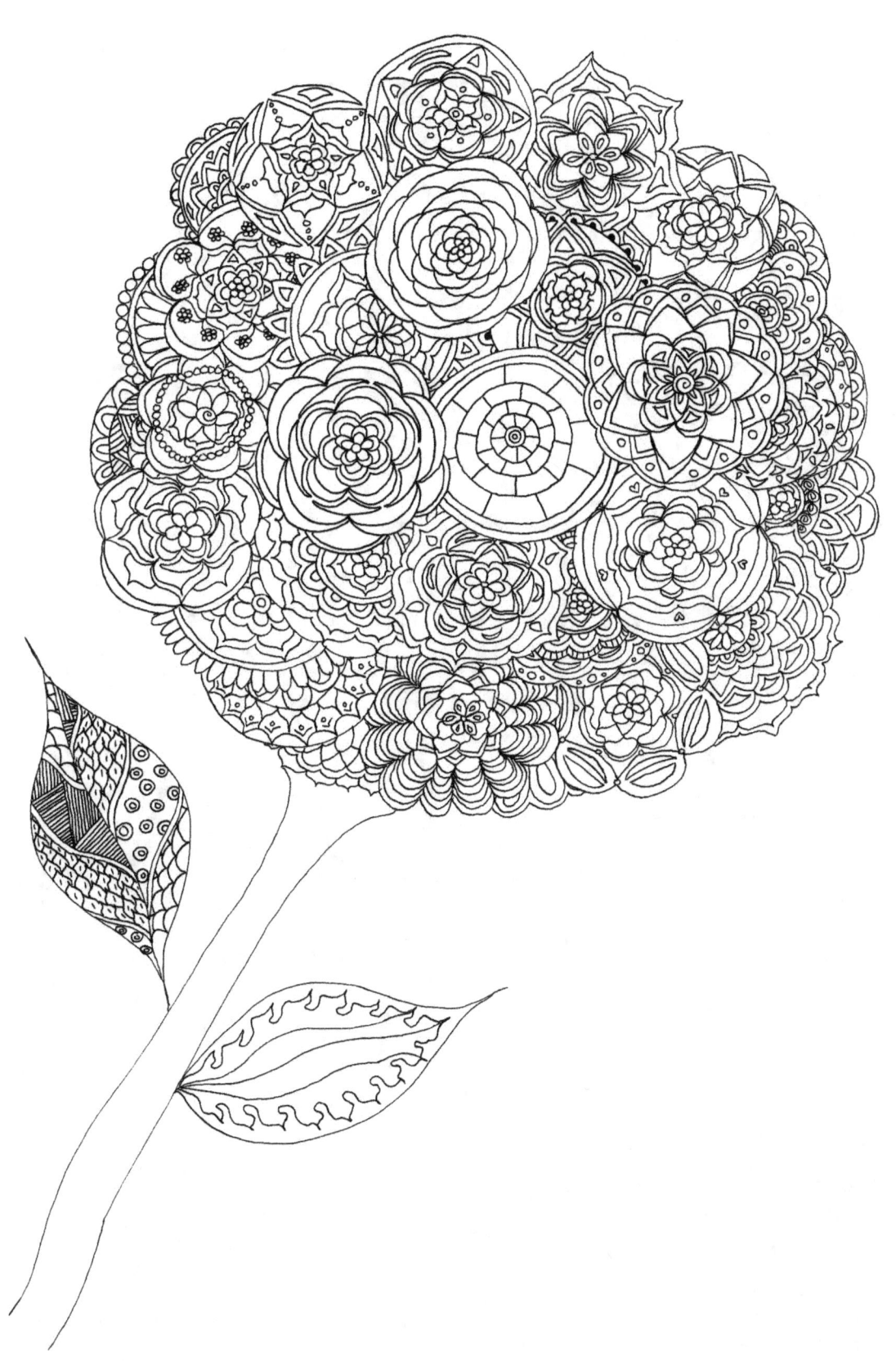

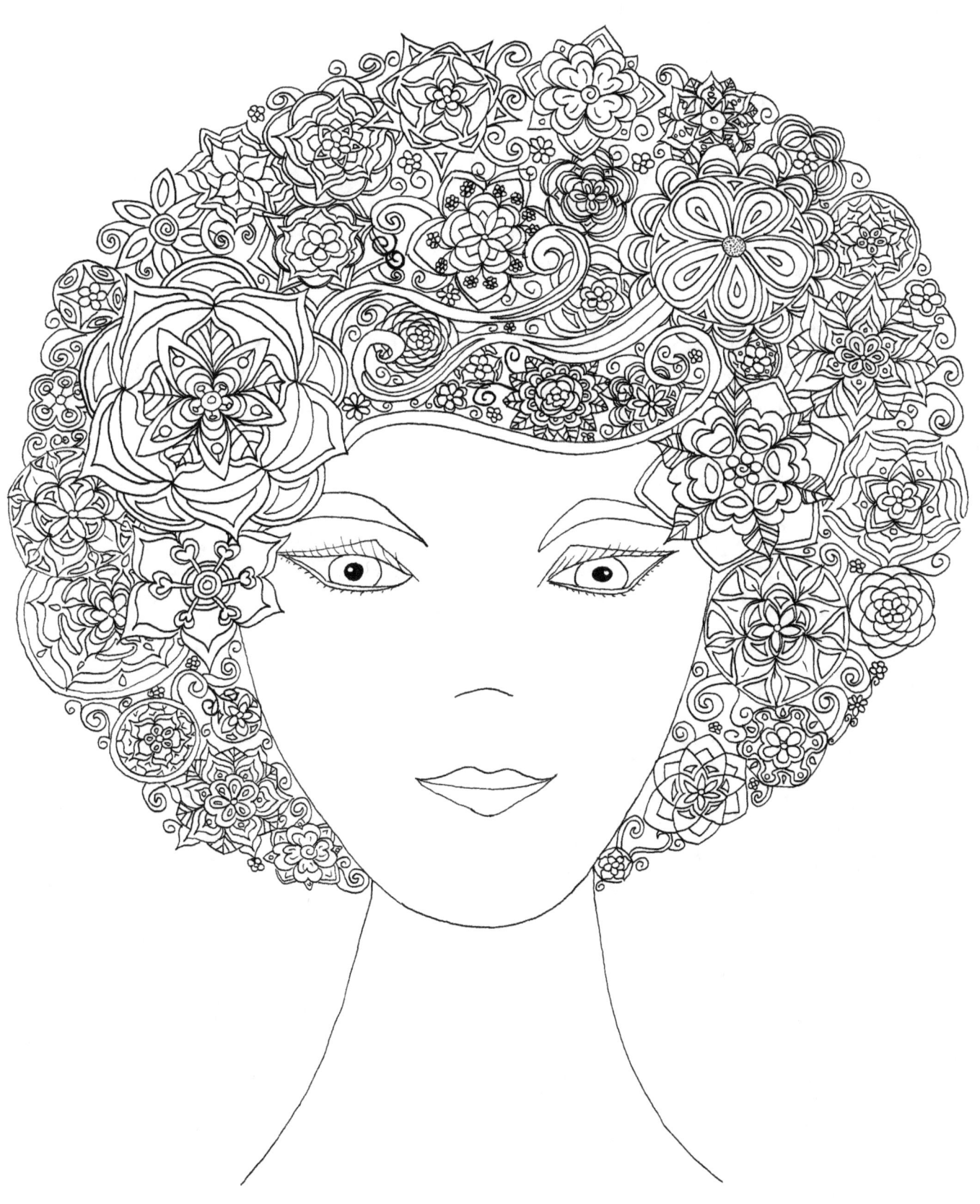

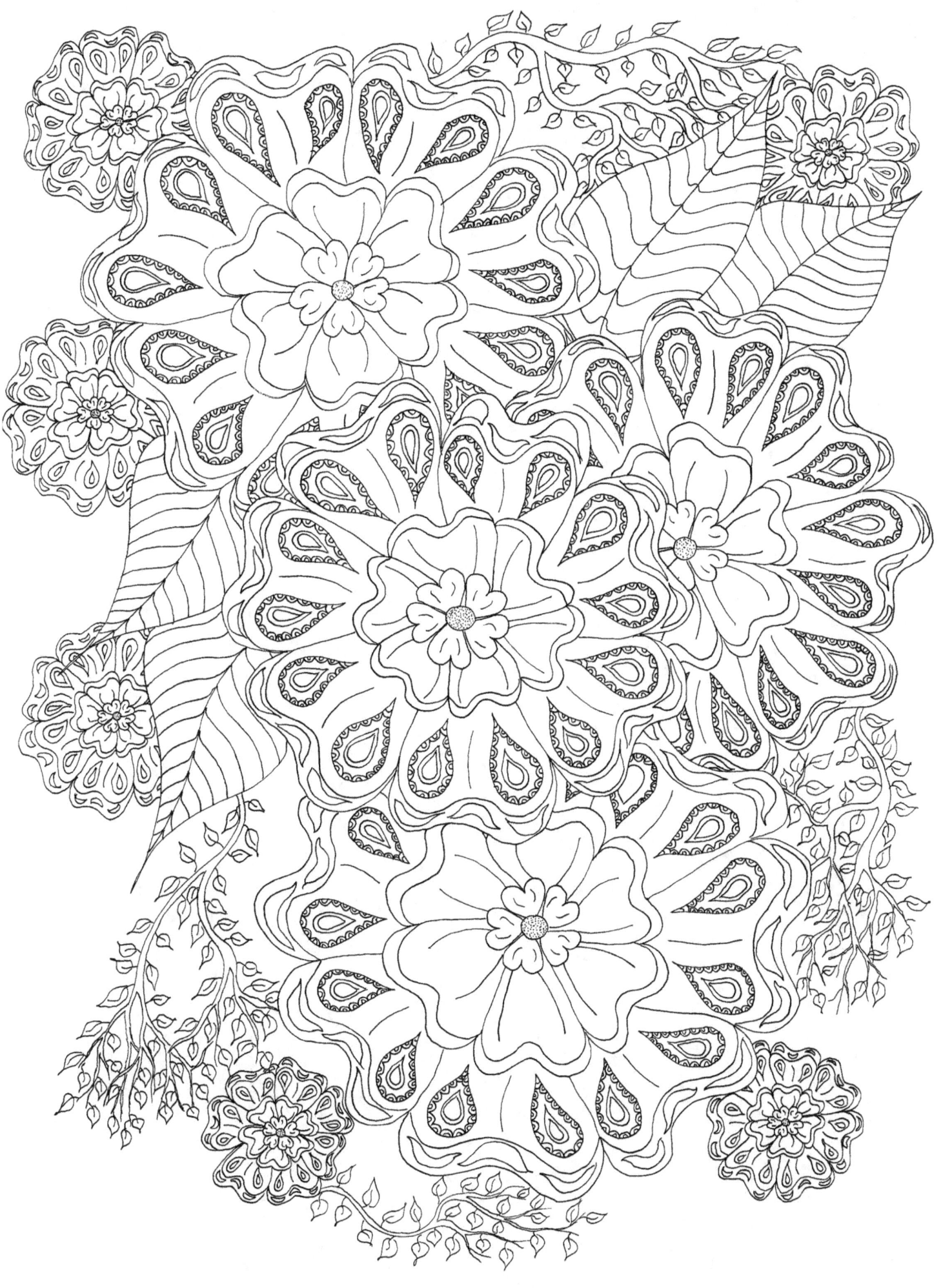

Contributing Artist
Lynne McGee
Brisbane, Australia

Facebook : Colorandtangle

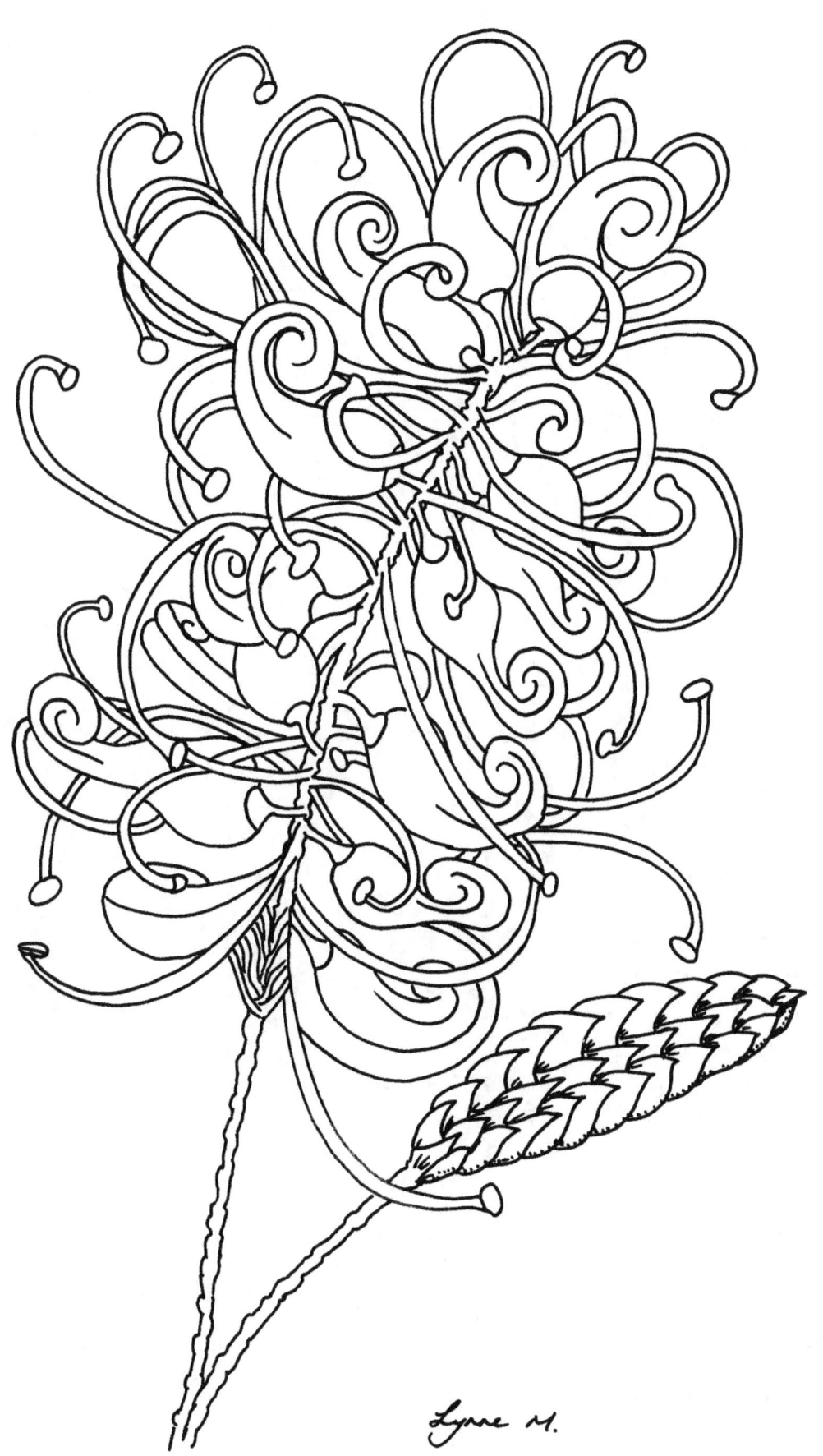

Lynne M.

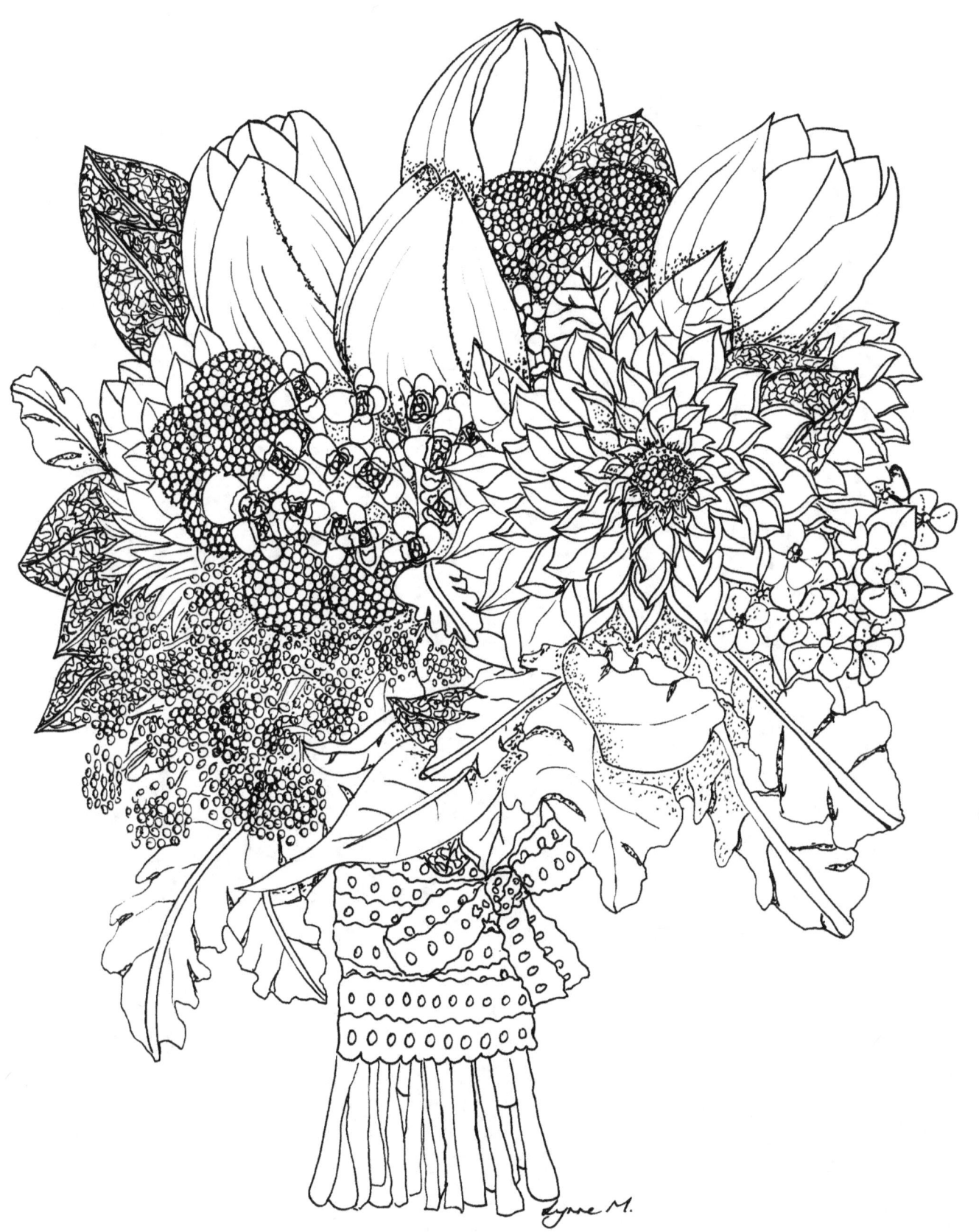

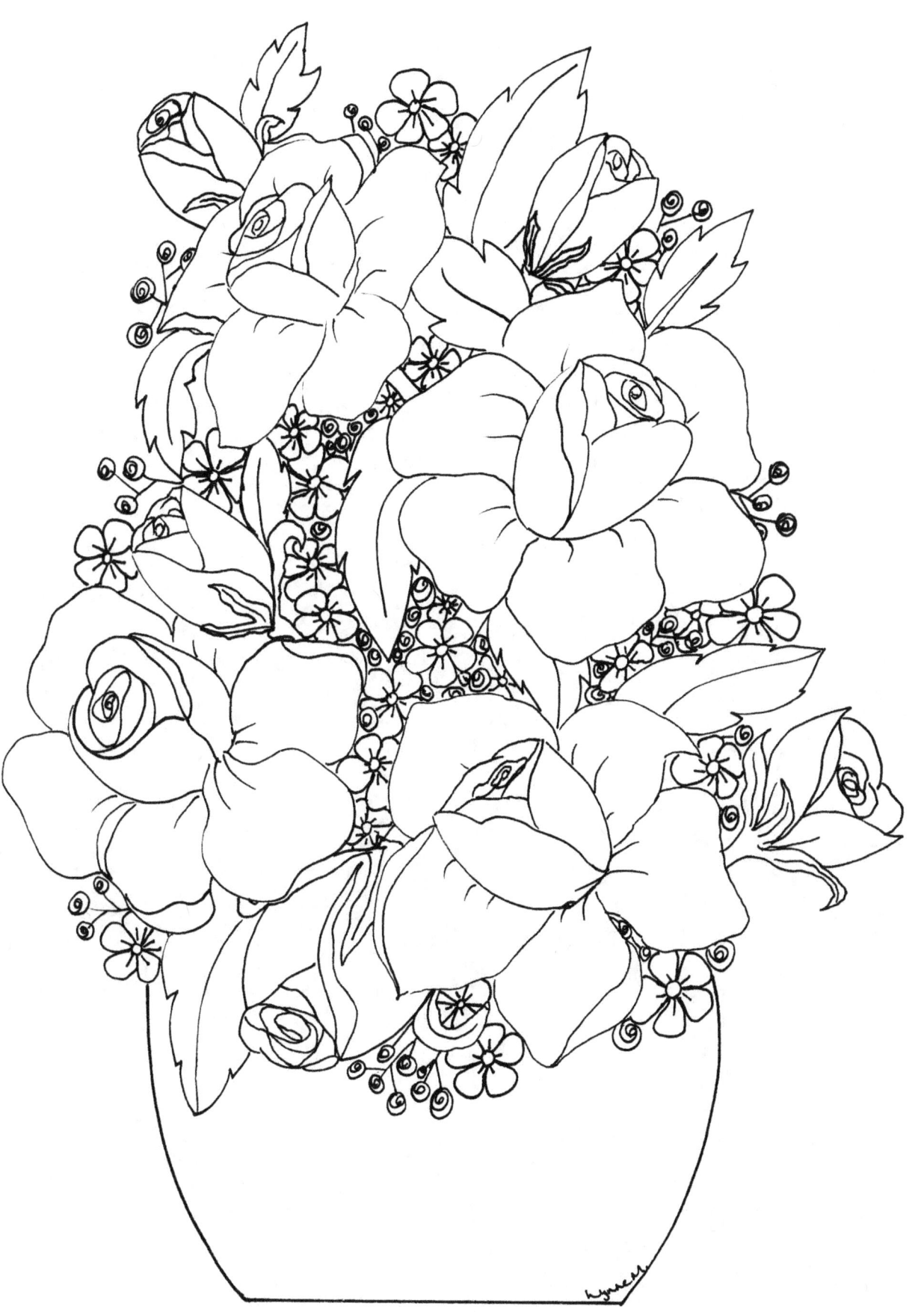

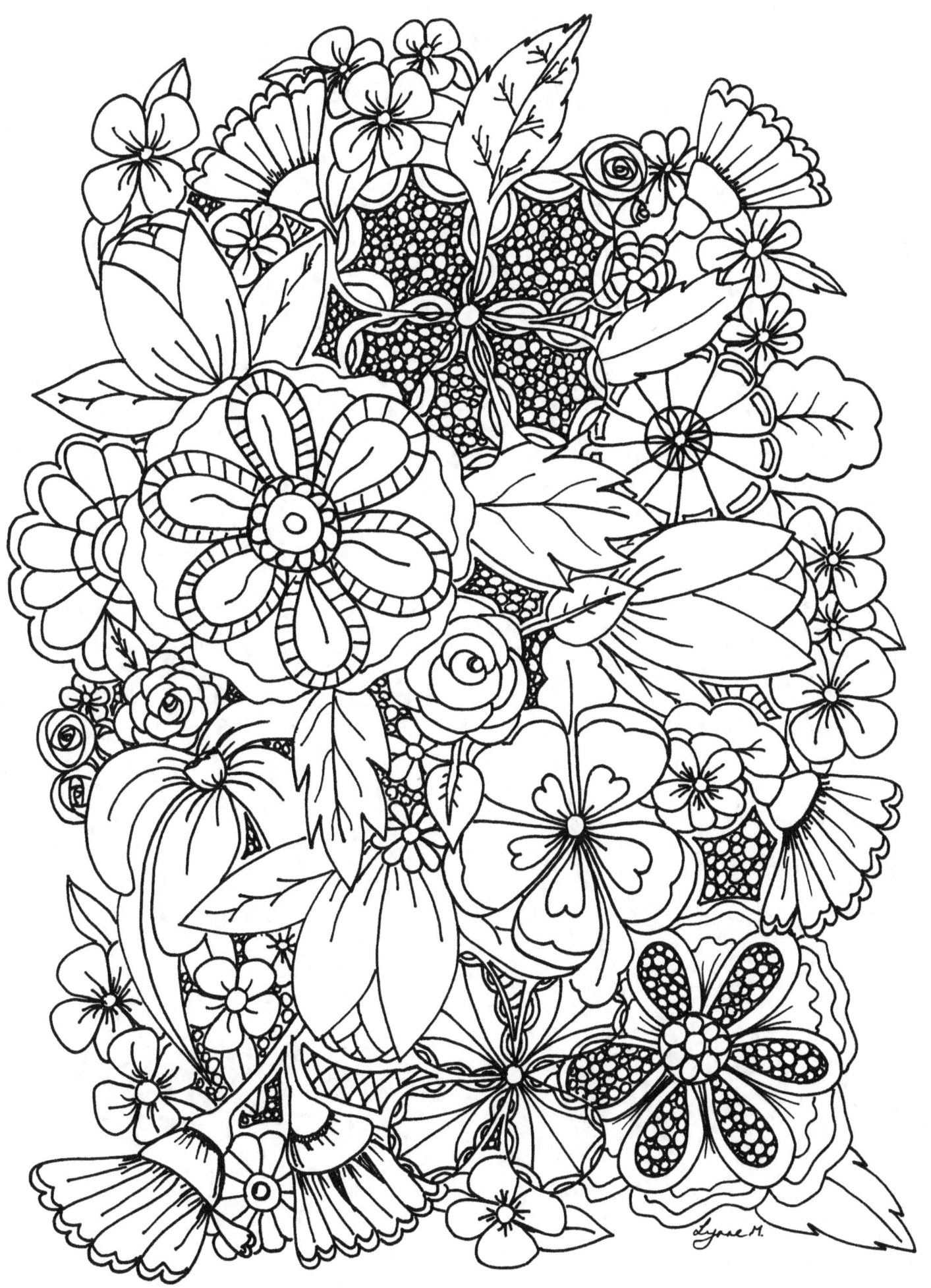

Contributing Artist
Peggy Sue's Artwork
The Netherlands

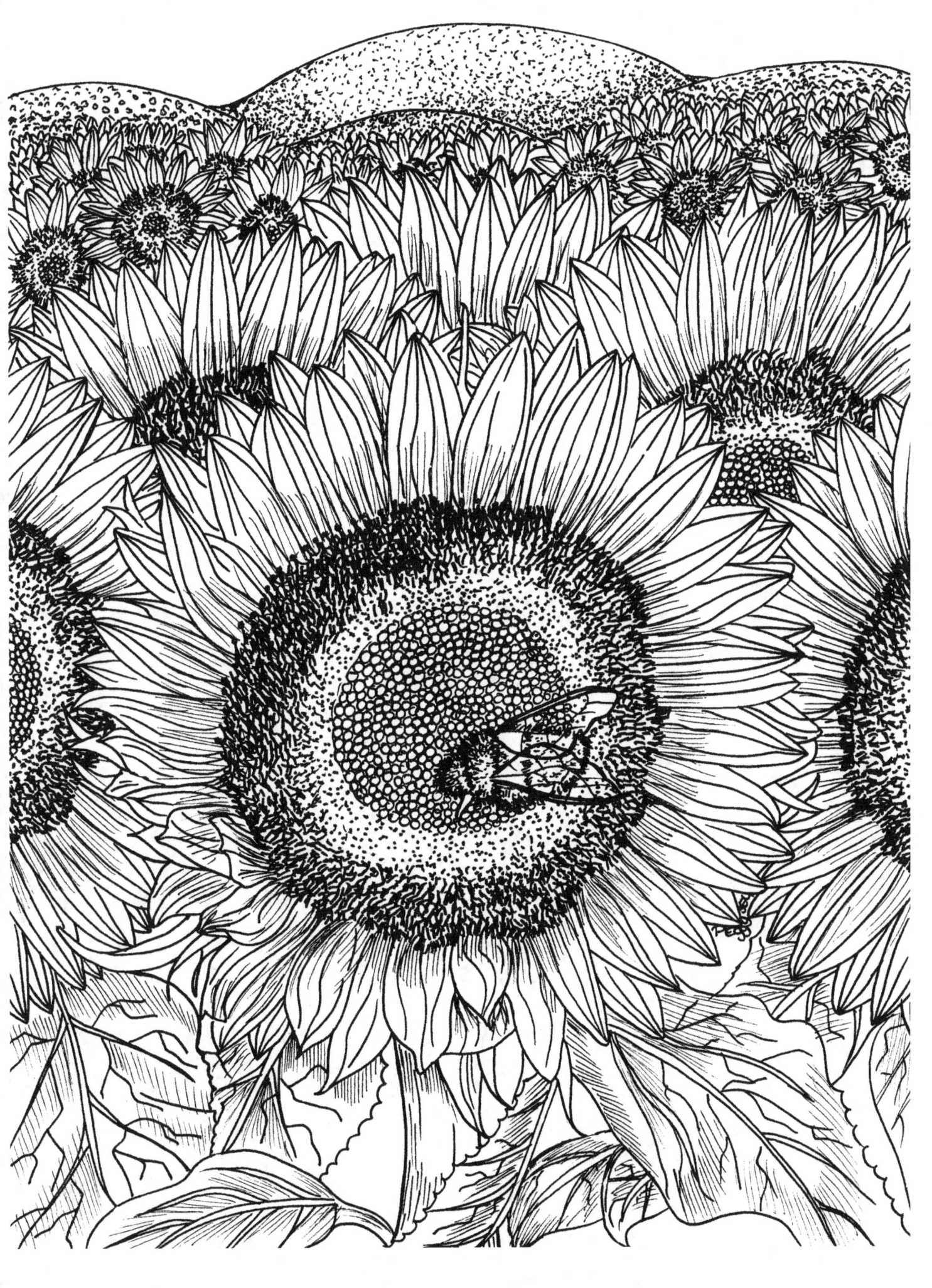

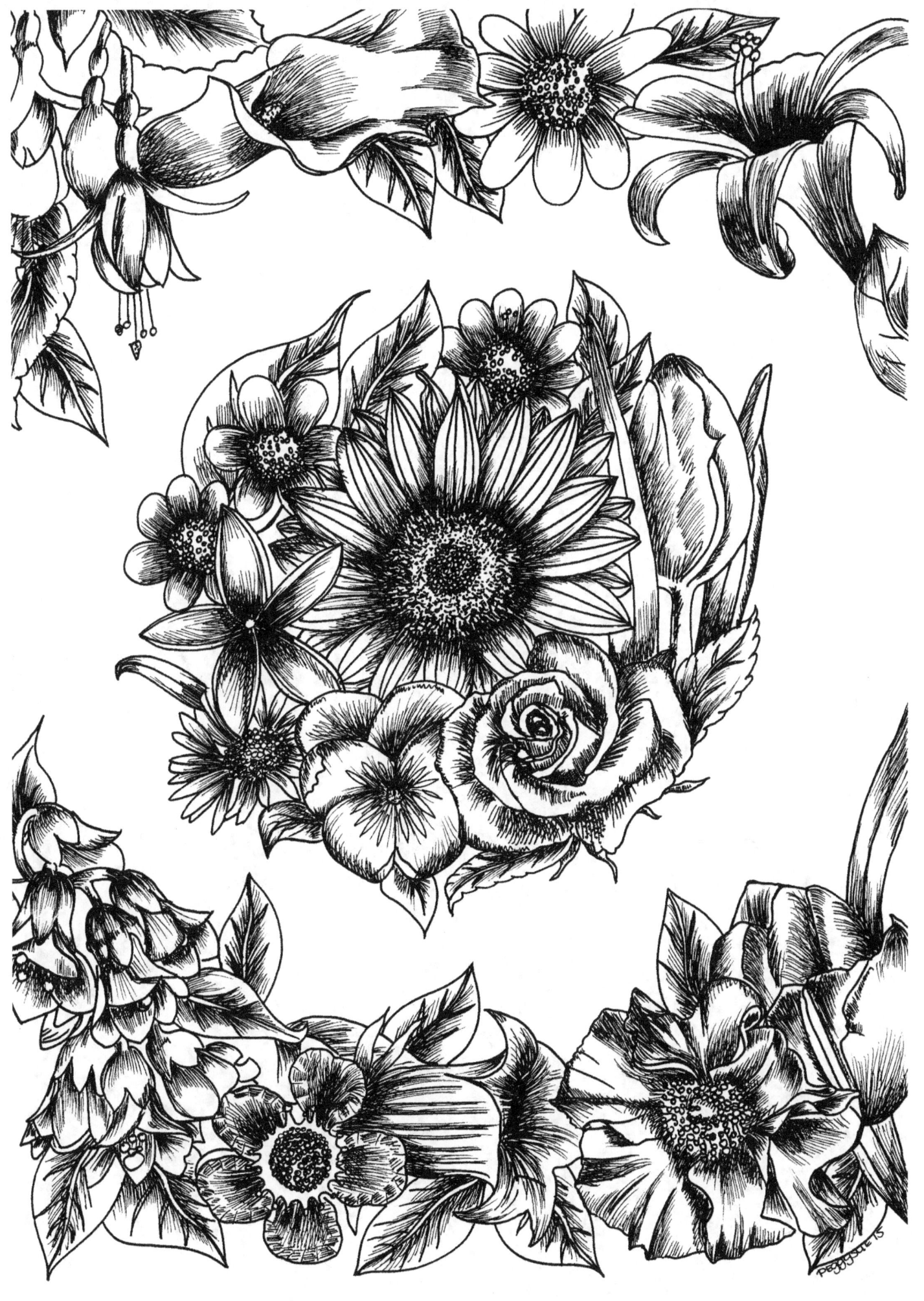

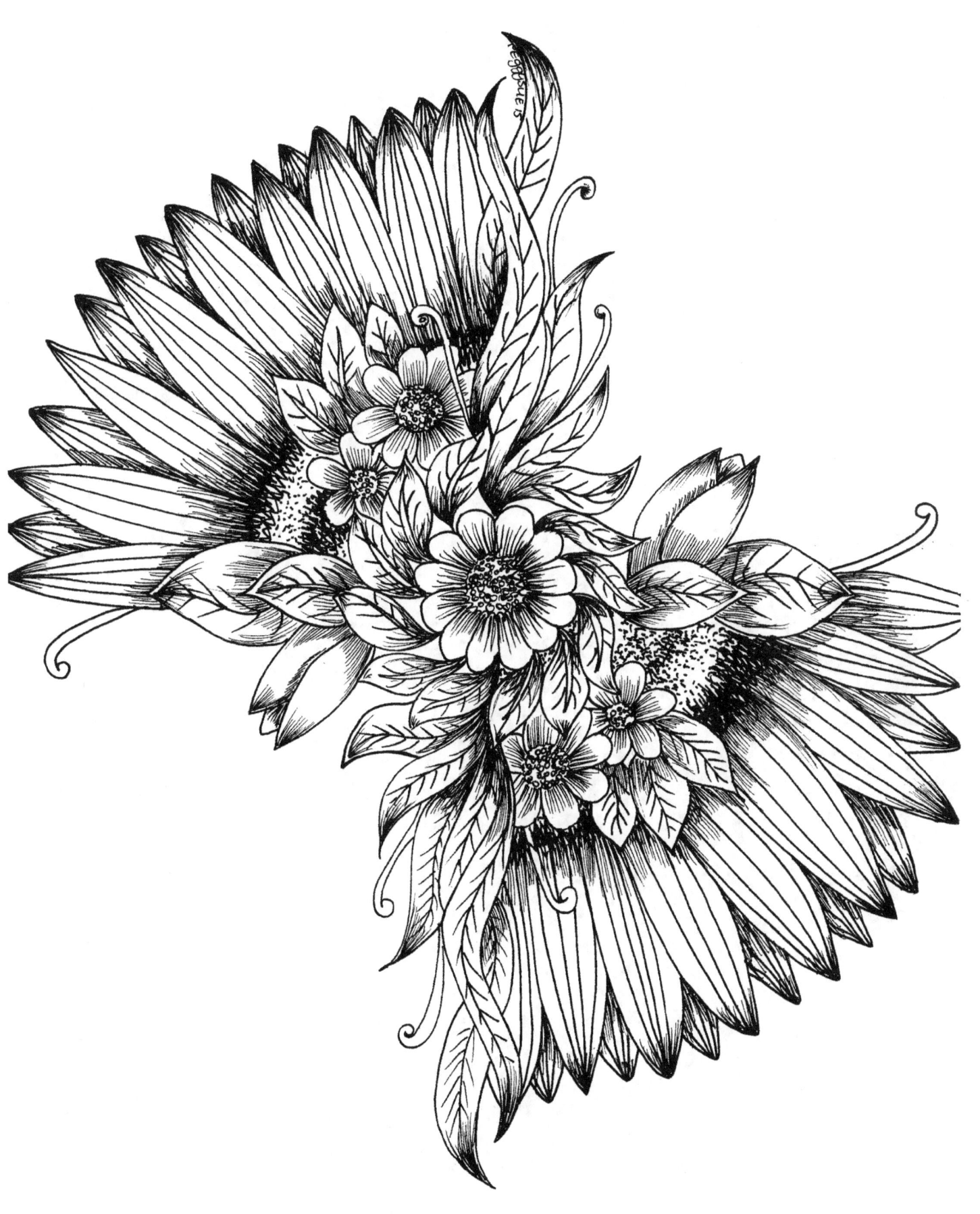

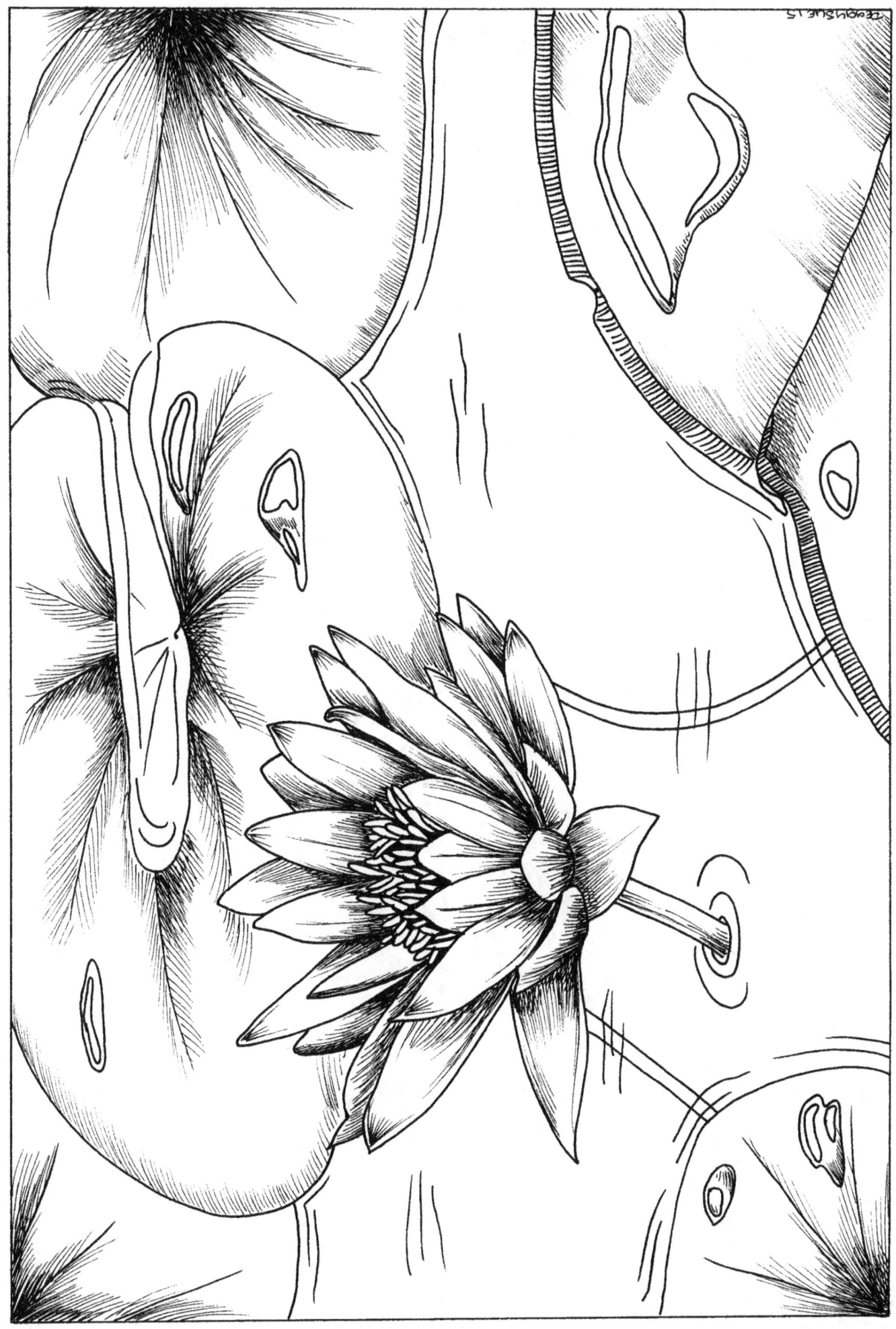

Contributing Artist
T.J.
USA

Facebook : TJsArtCorner

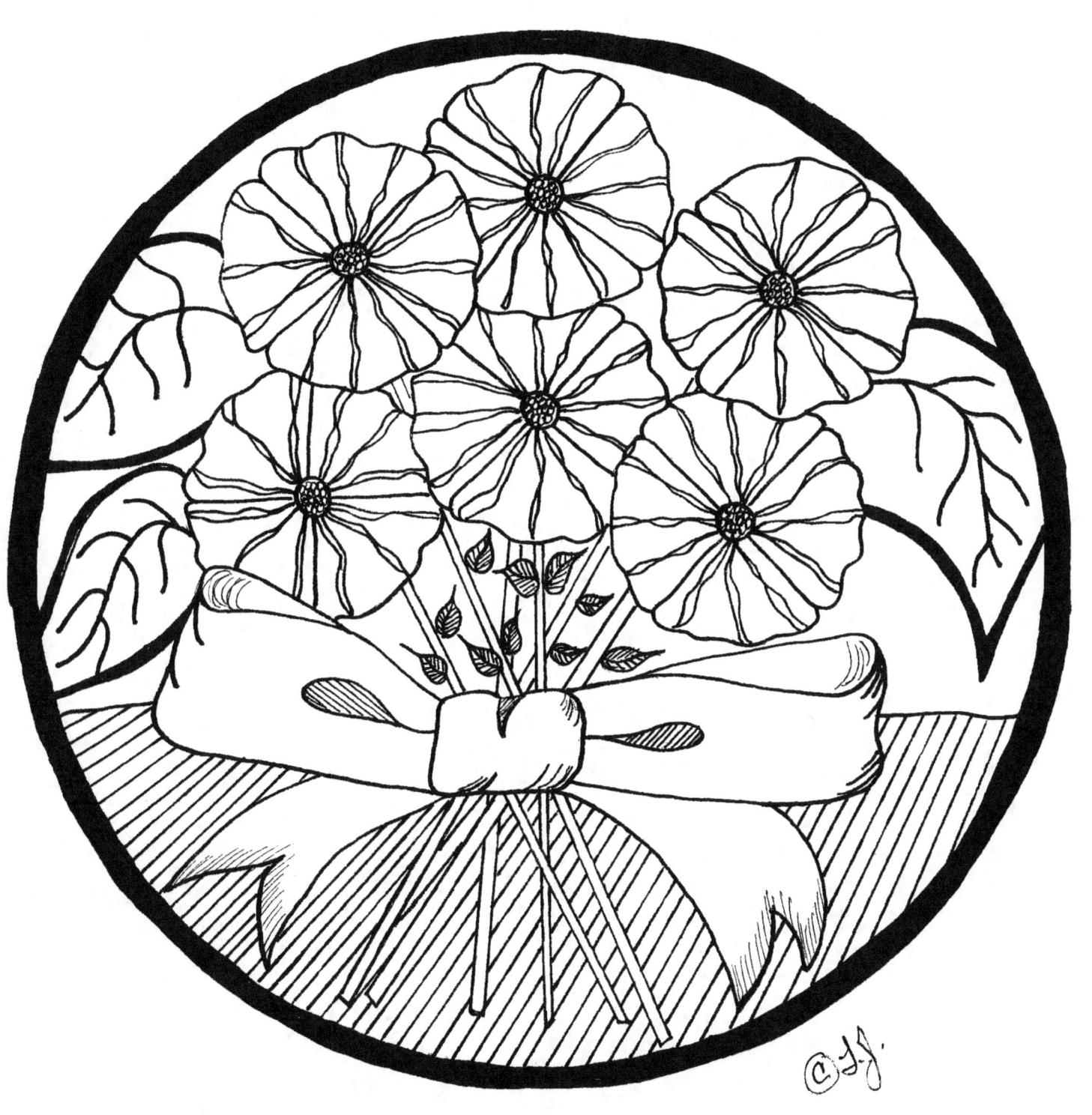

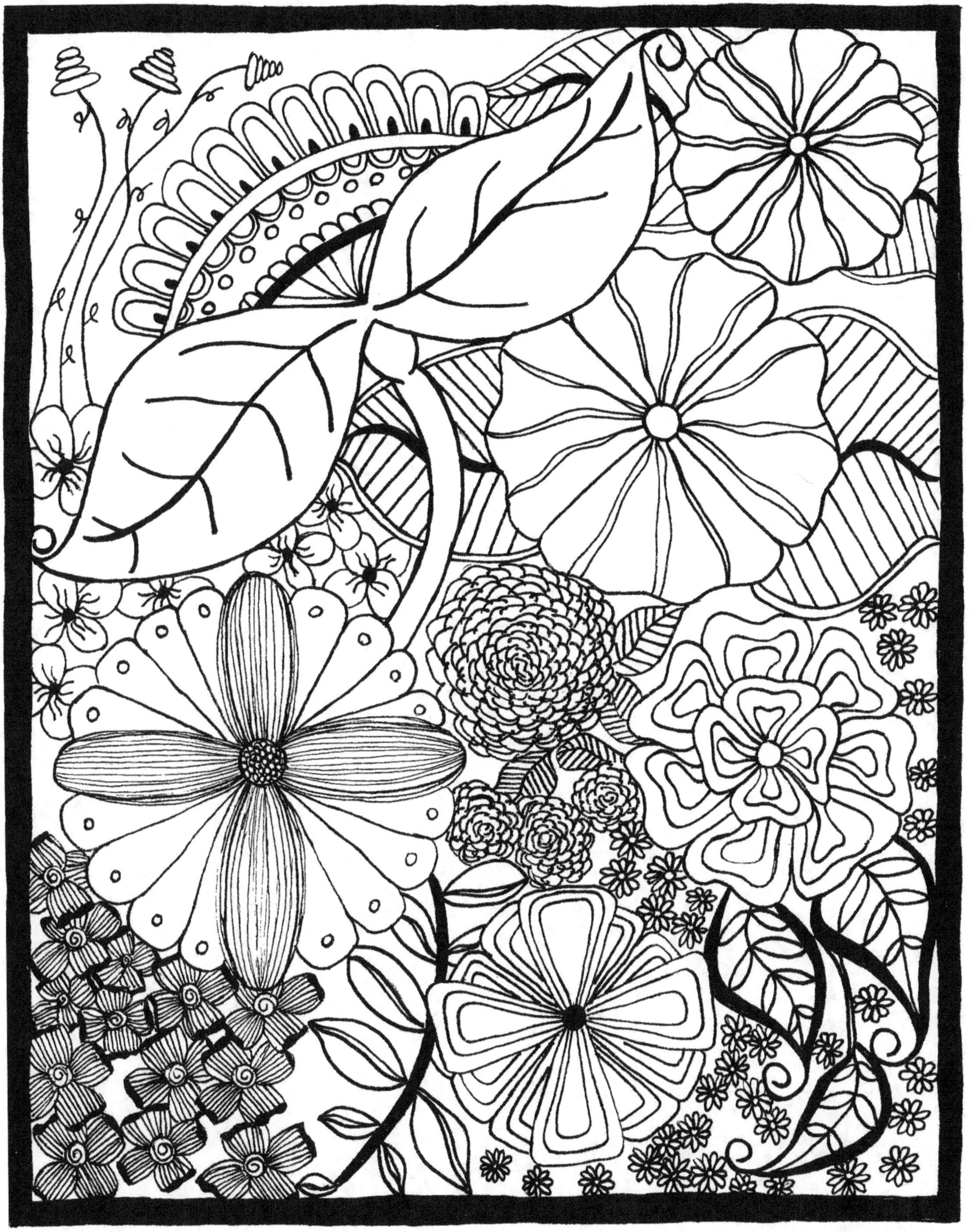

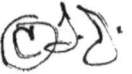

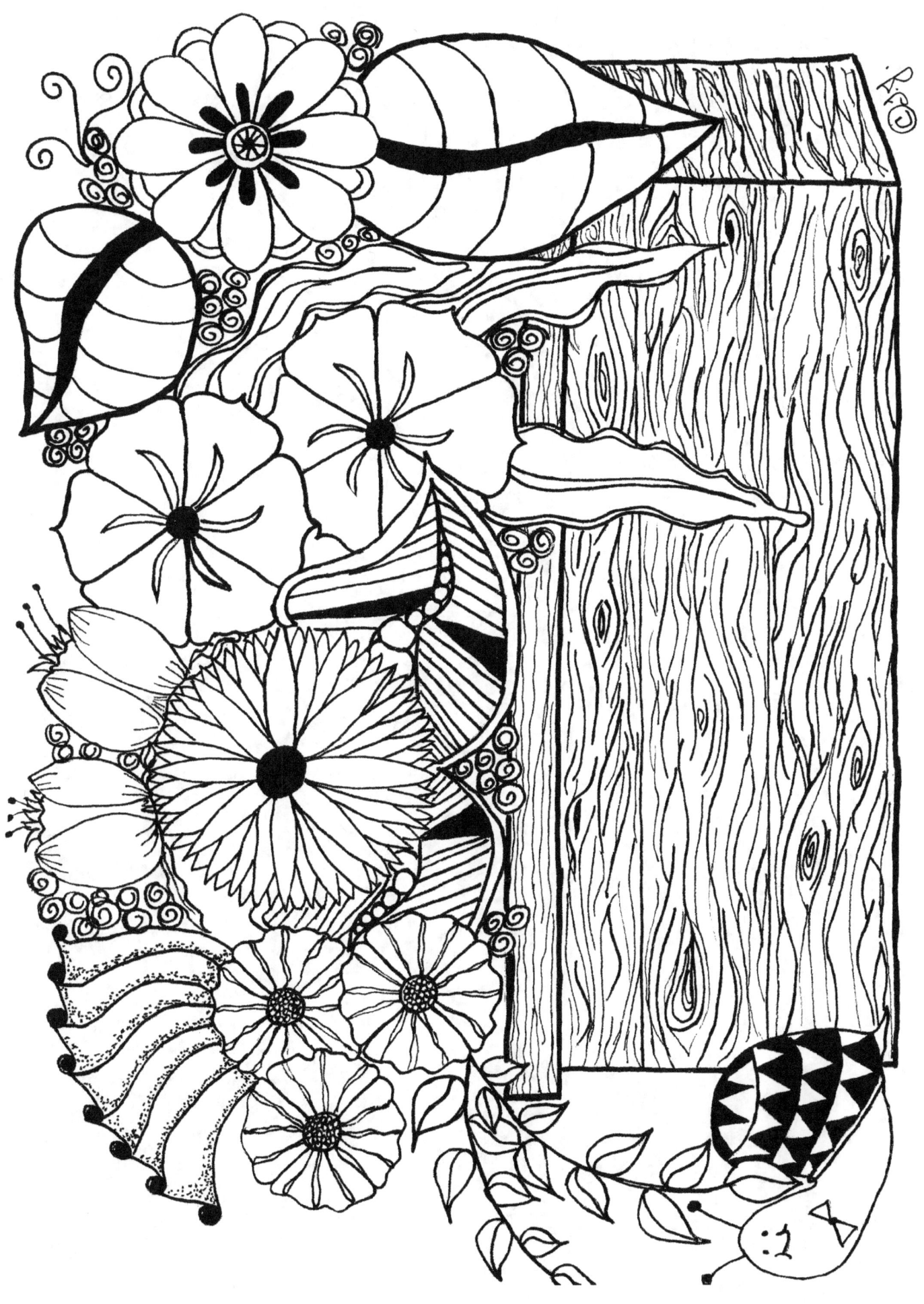

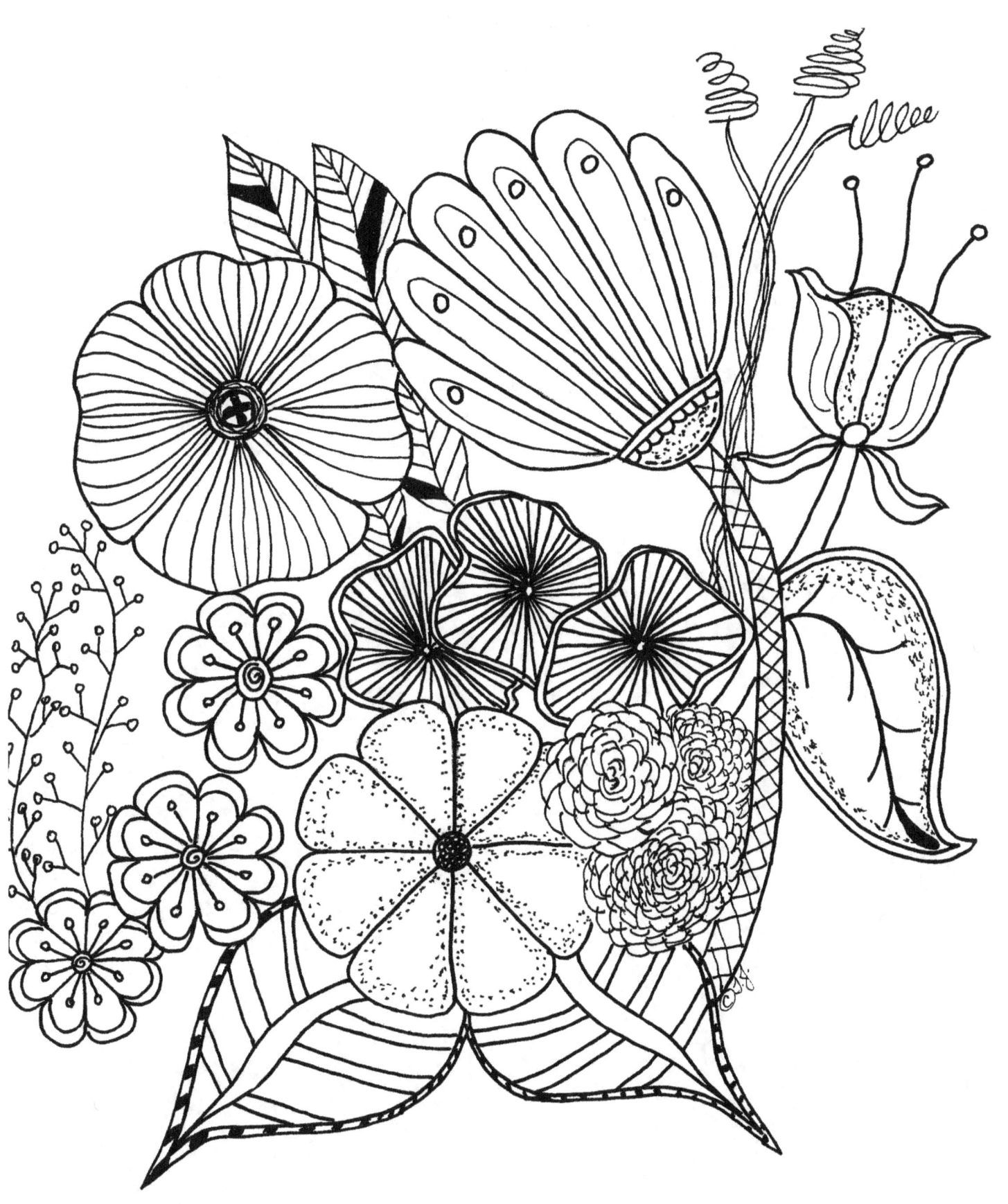

Contributing Artist
Iben Lykke Højholdt
Denmark

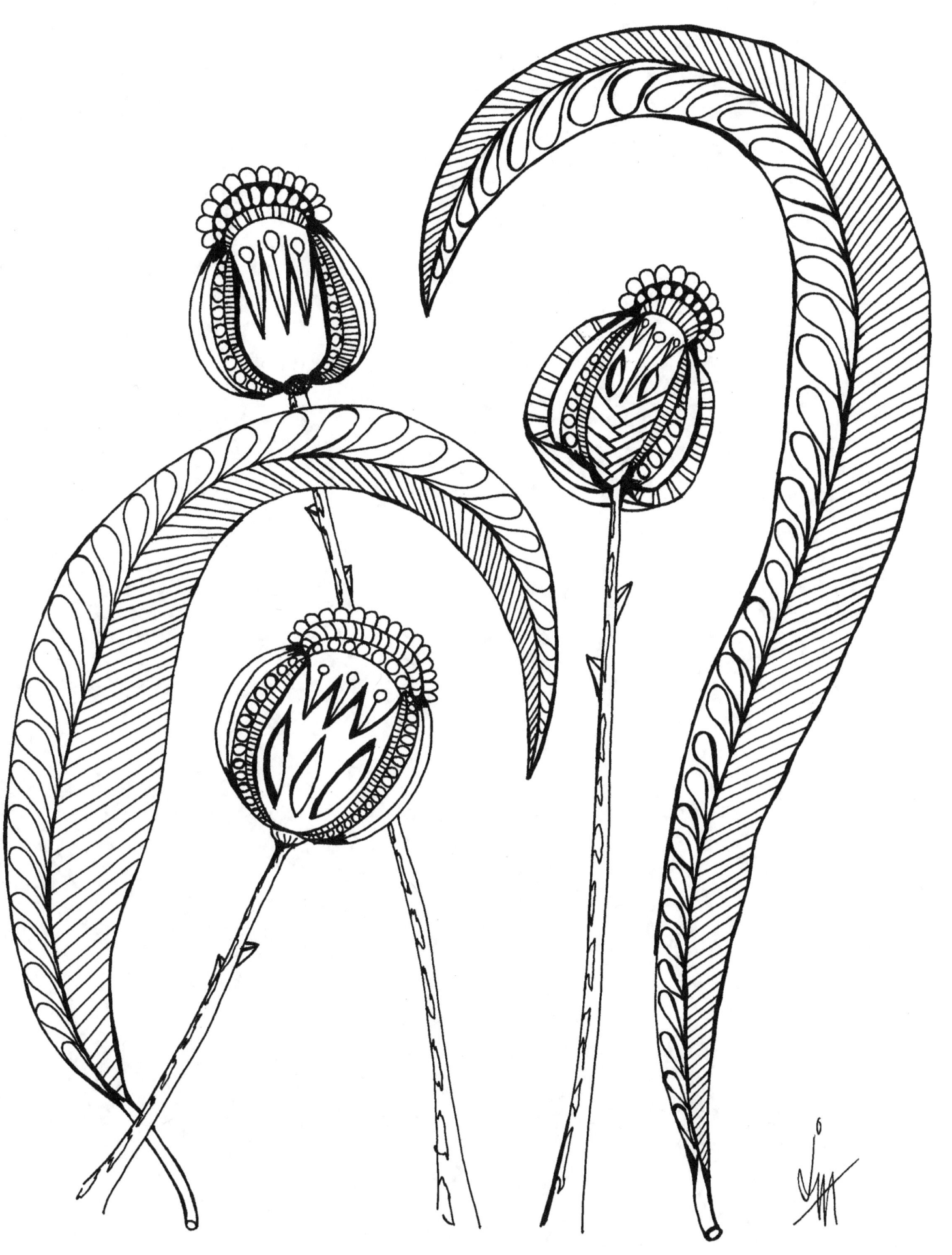

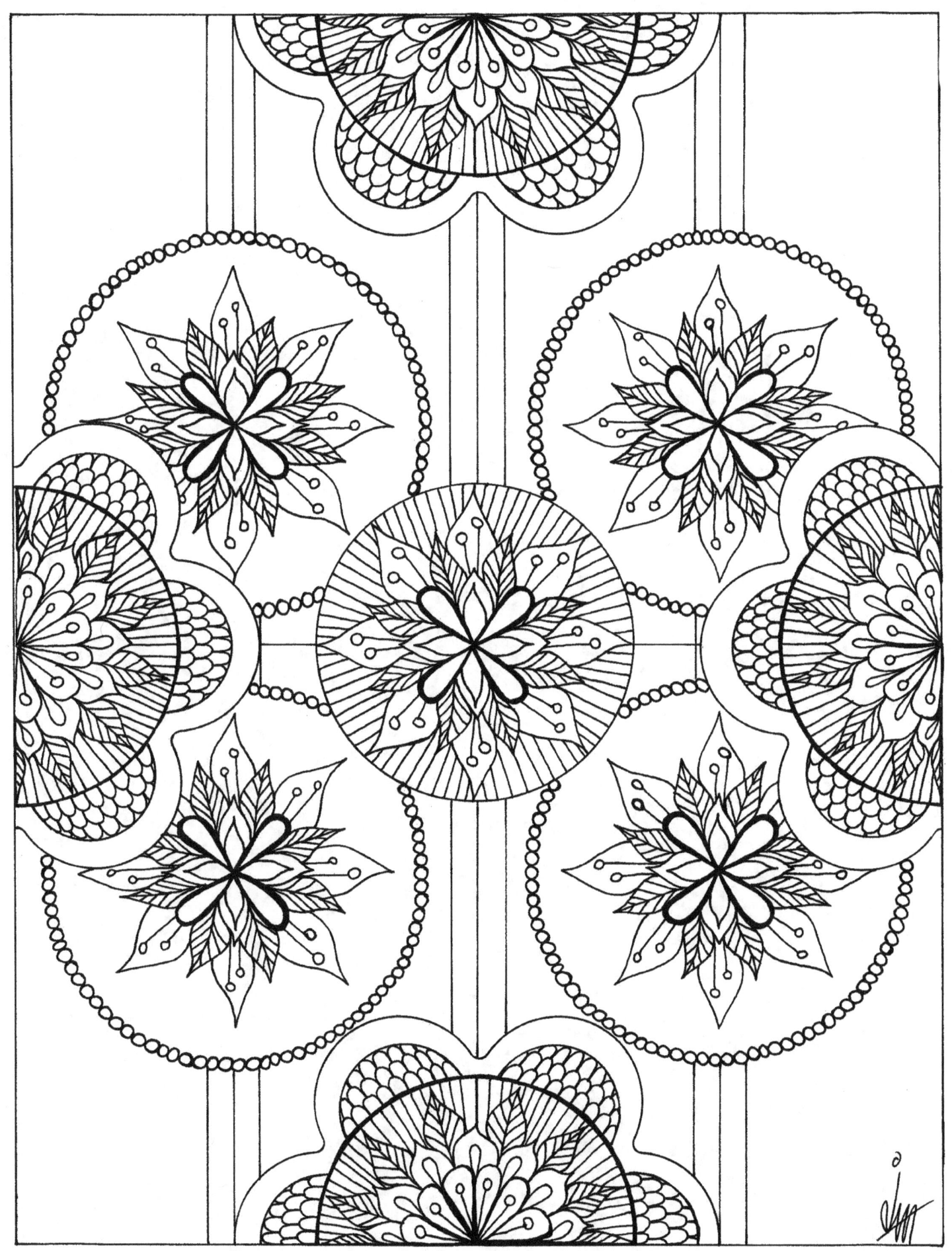

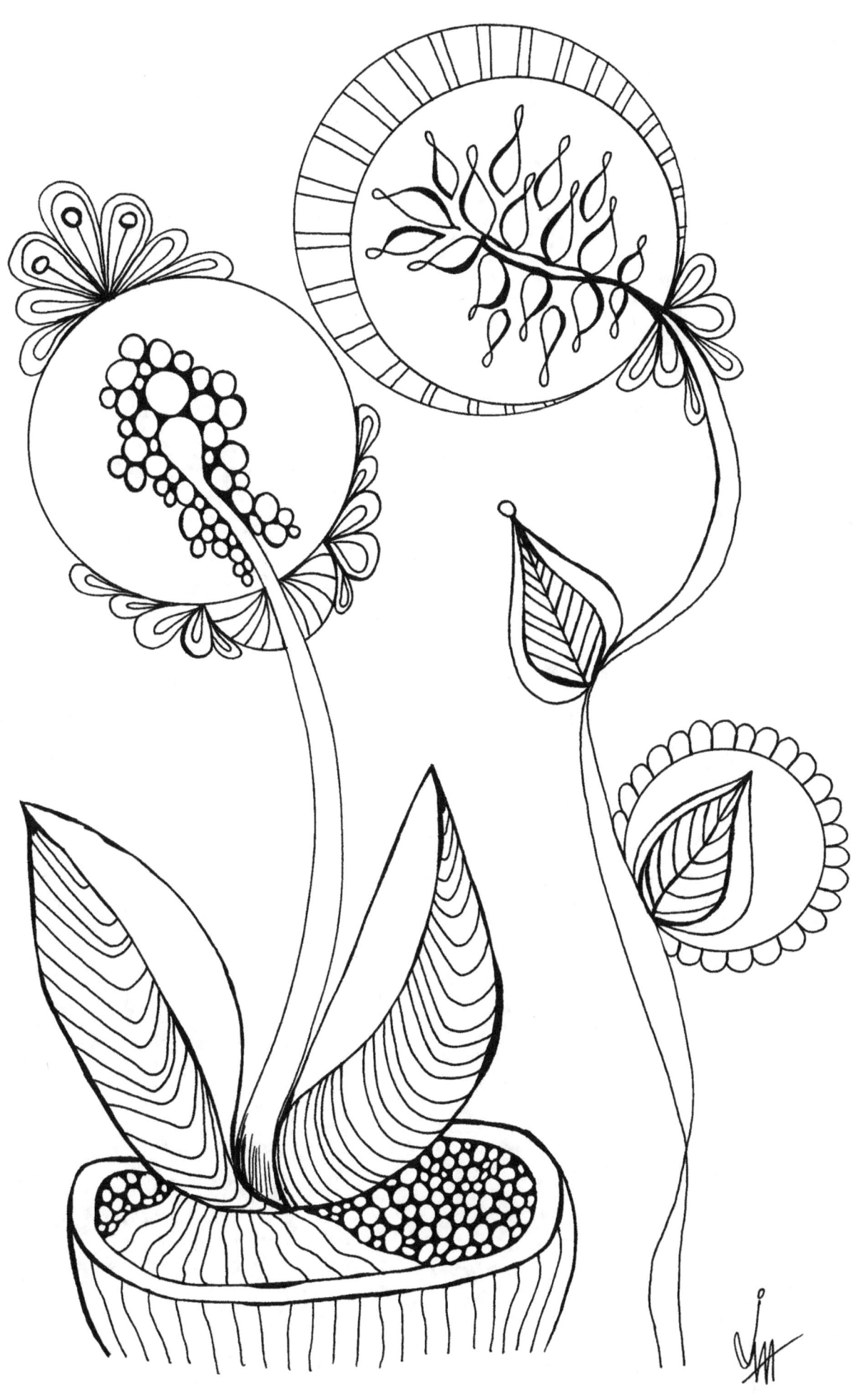

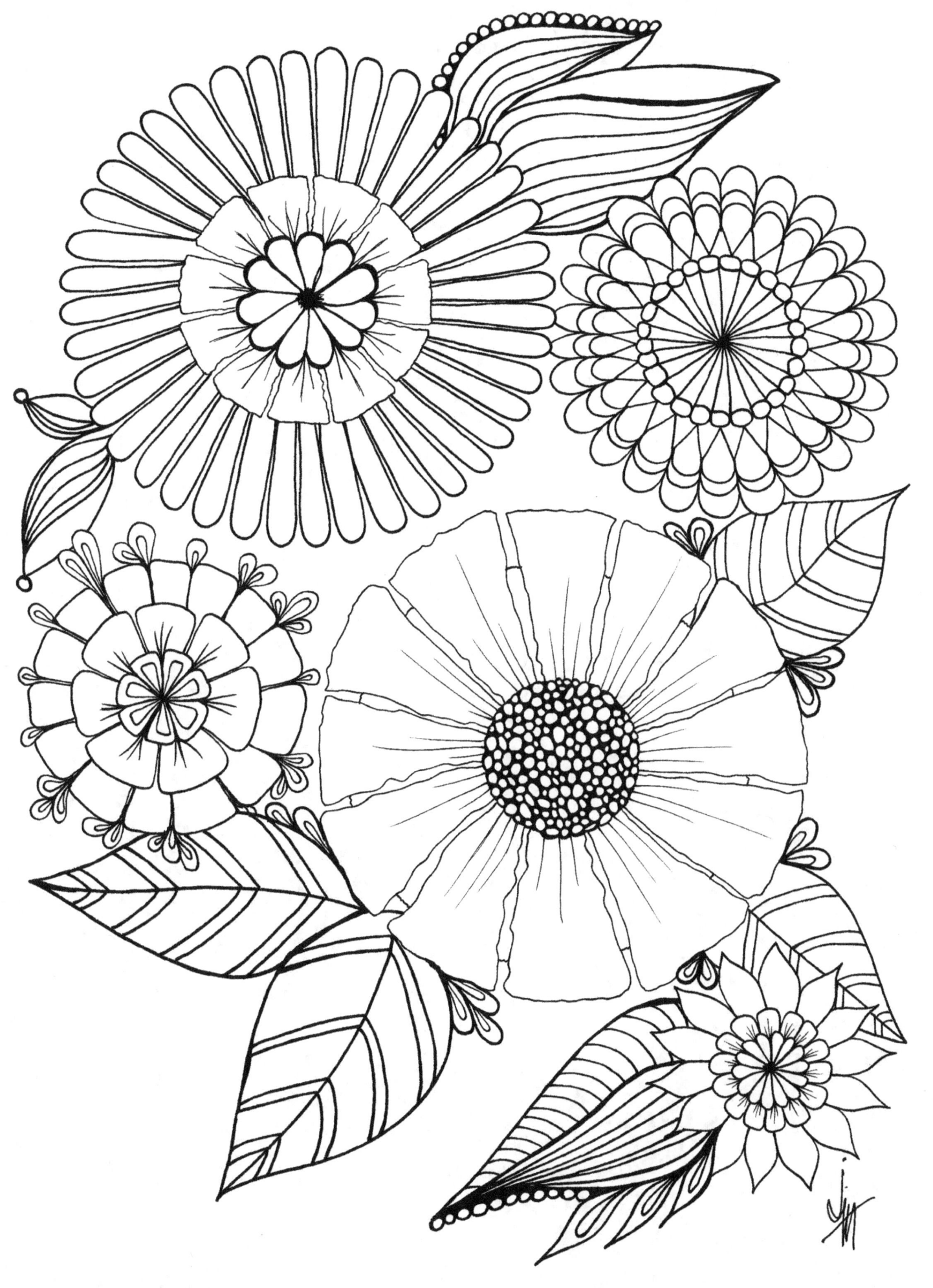

Contributing Artist
Gloria A. Lenzen
USA

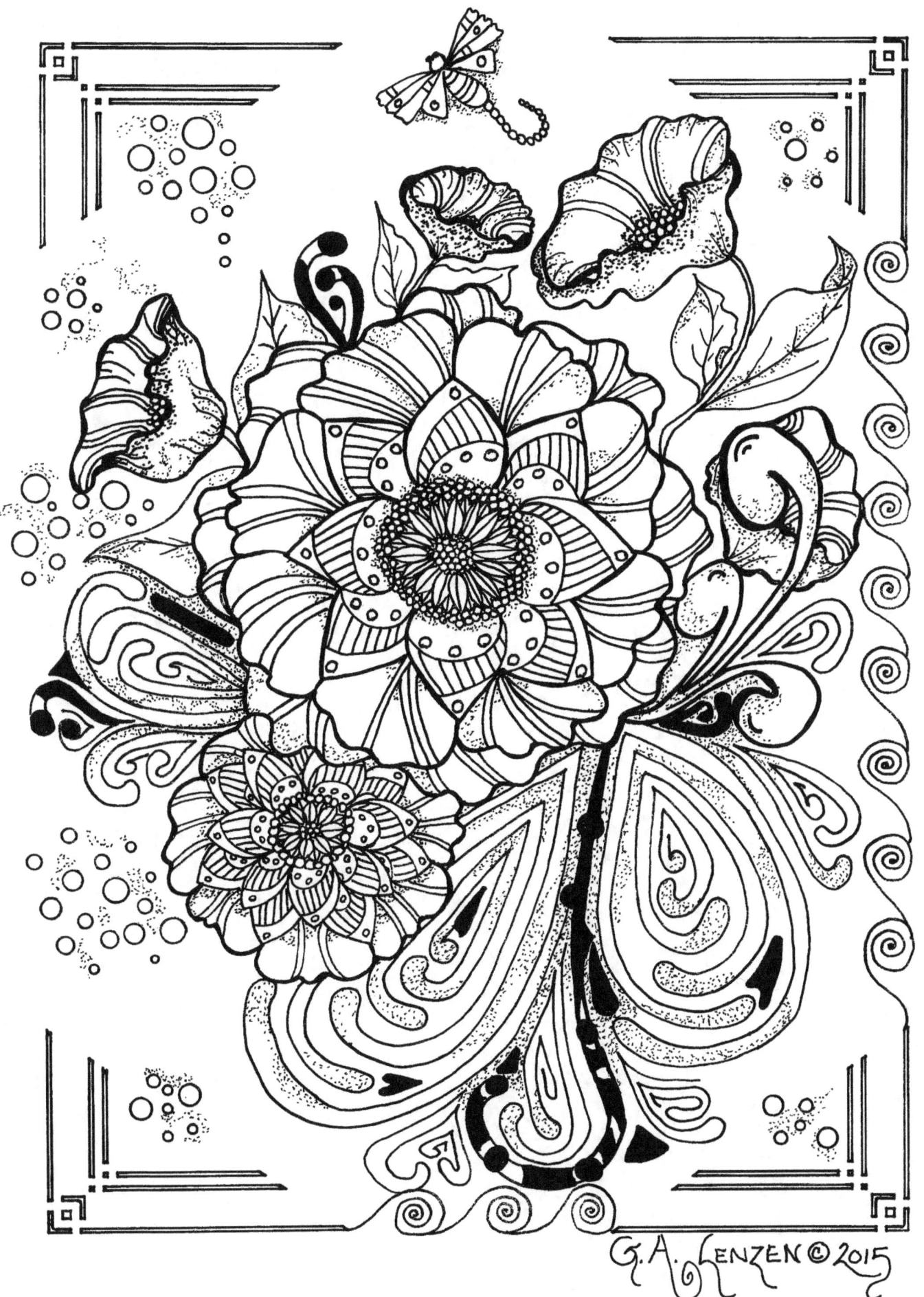

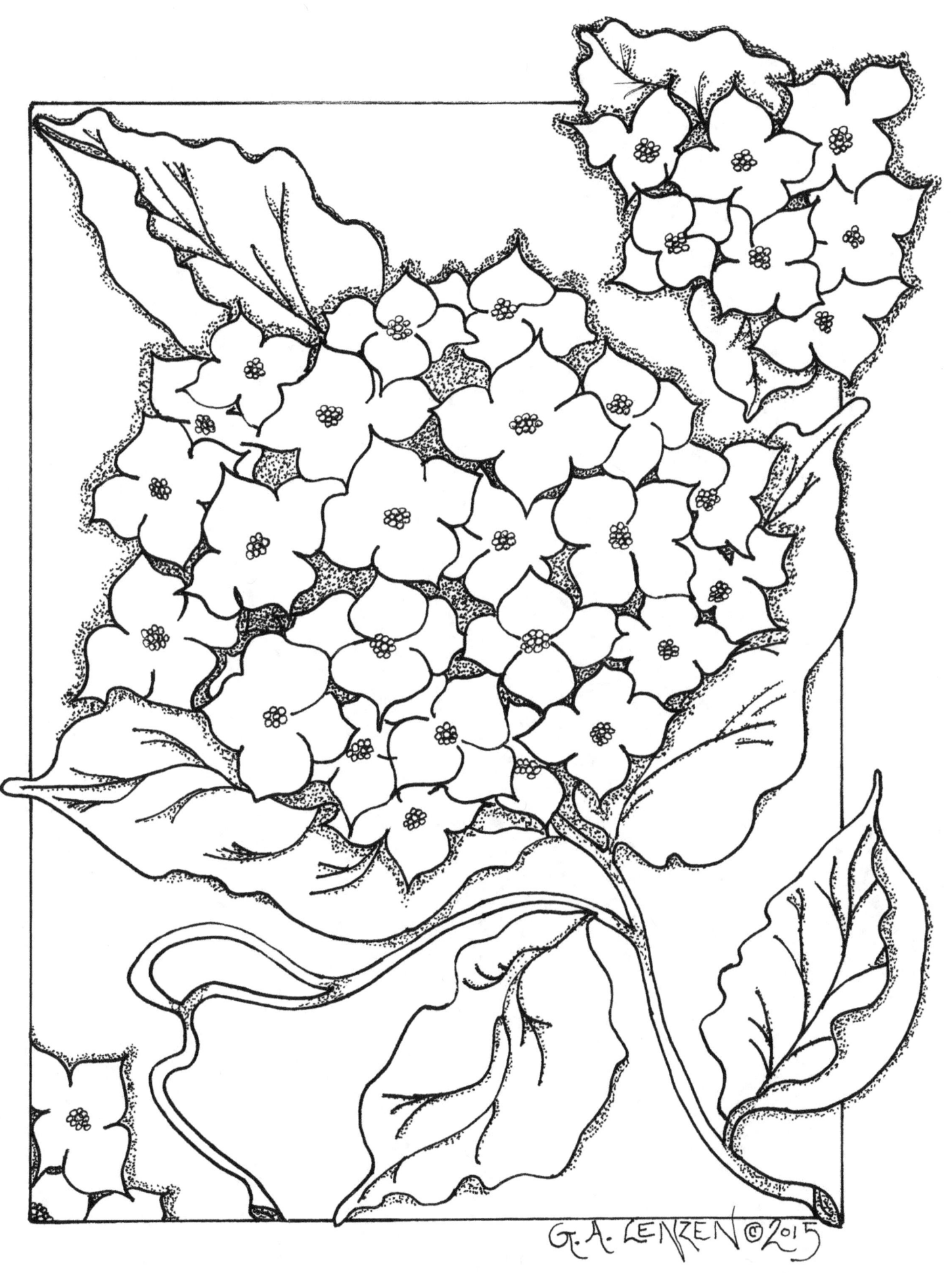

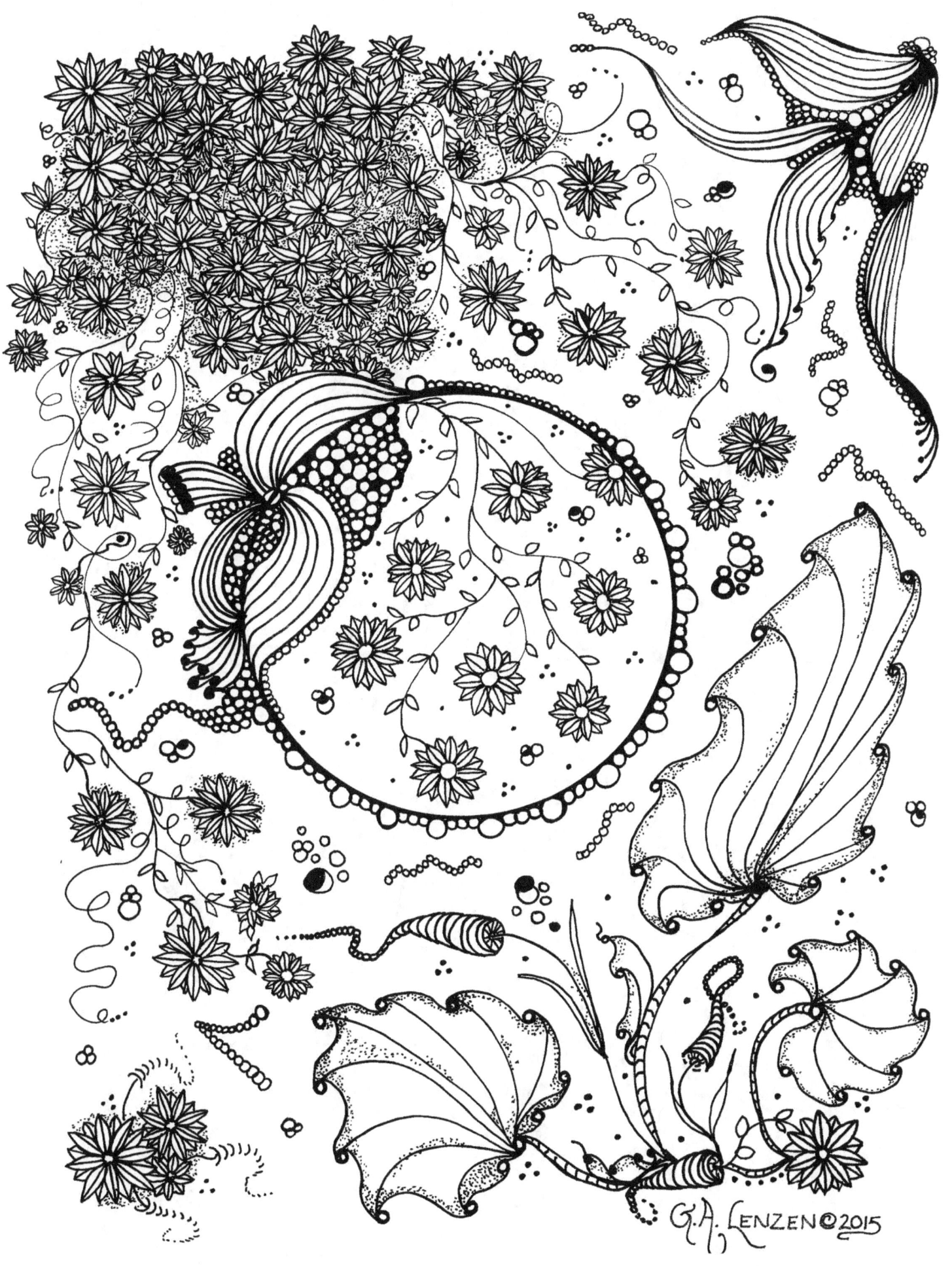

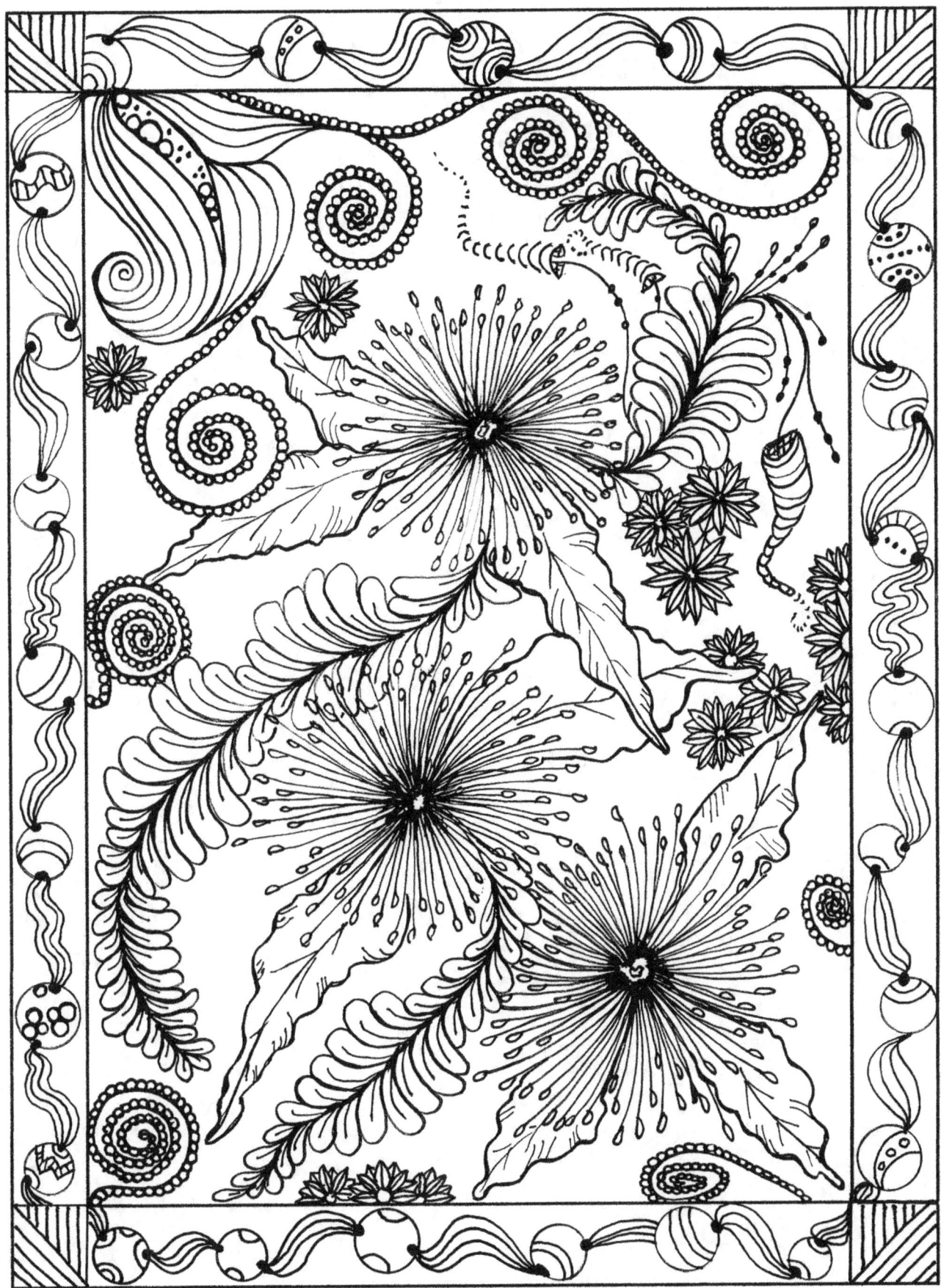

Contributing Artist
Maud Feral Chauveau
(MFC)
France

« MFC - Peinture, graphisme & illustration »

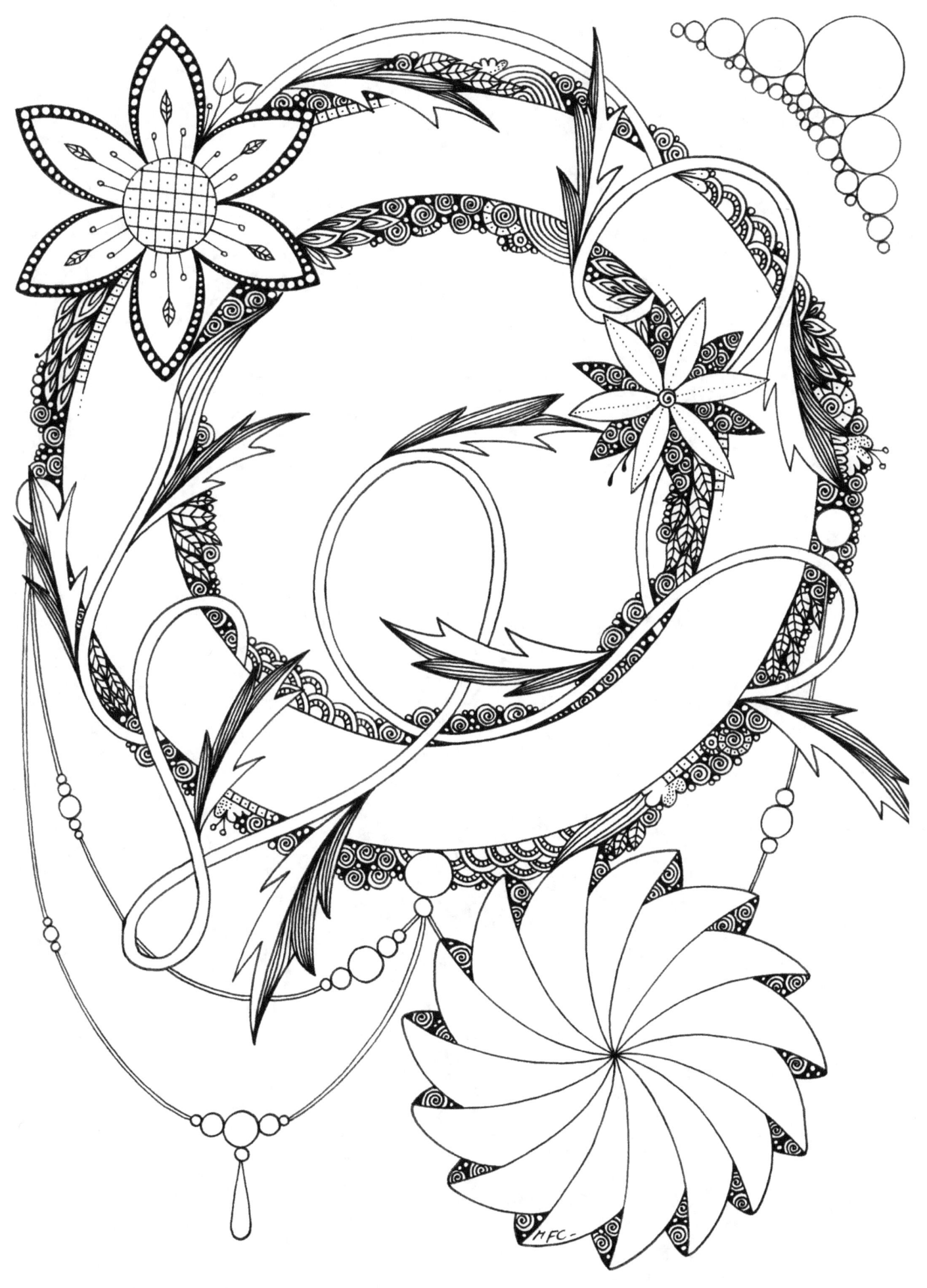

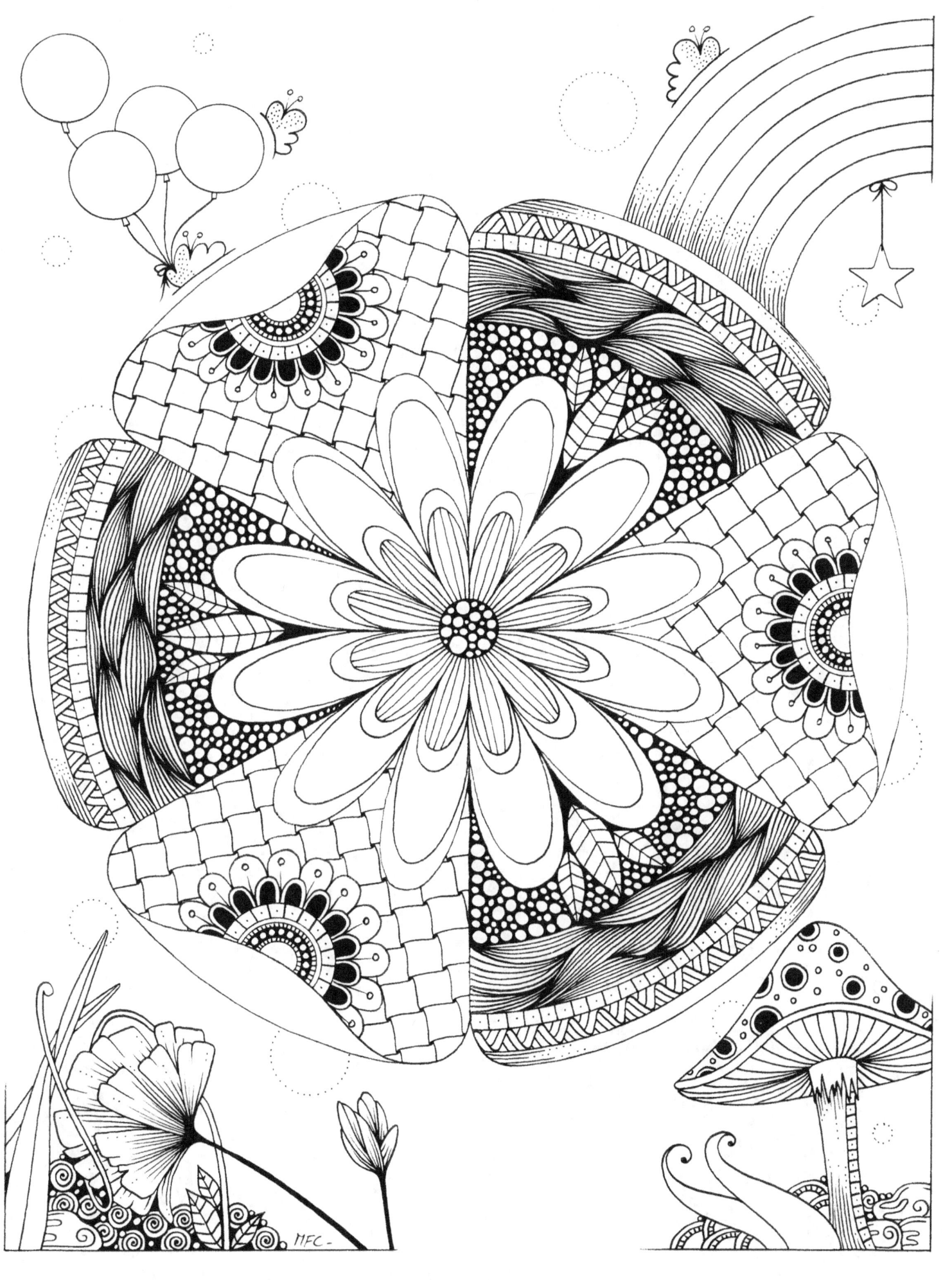

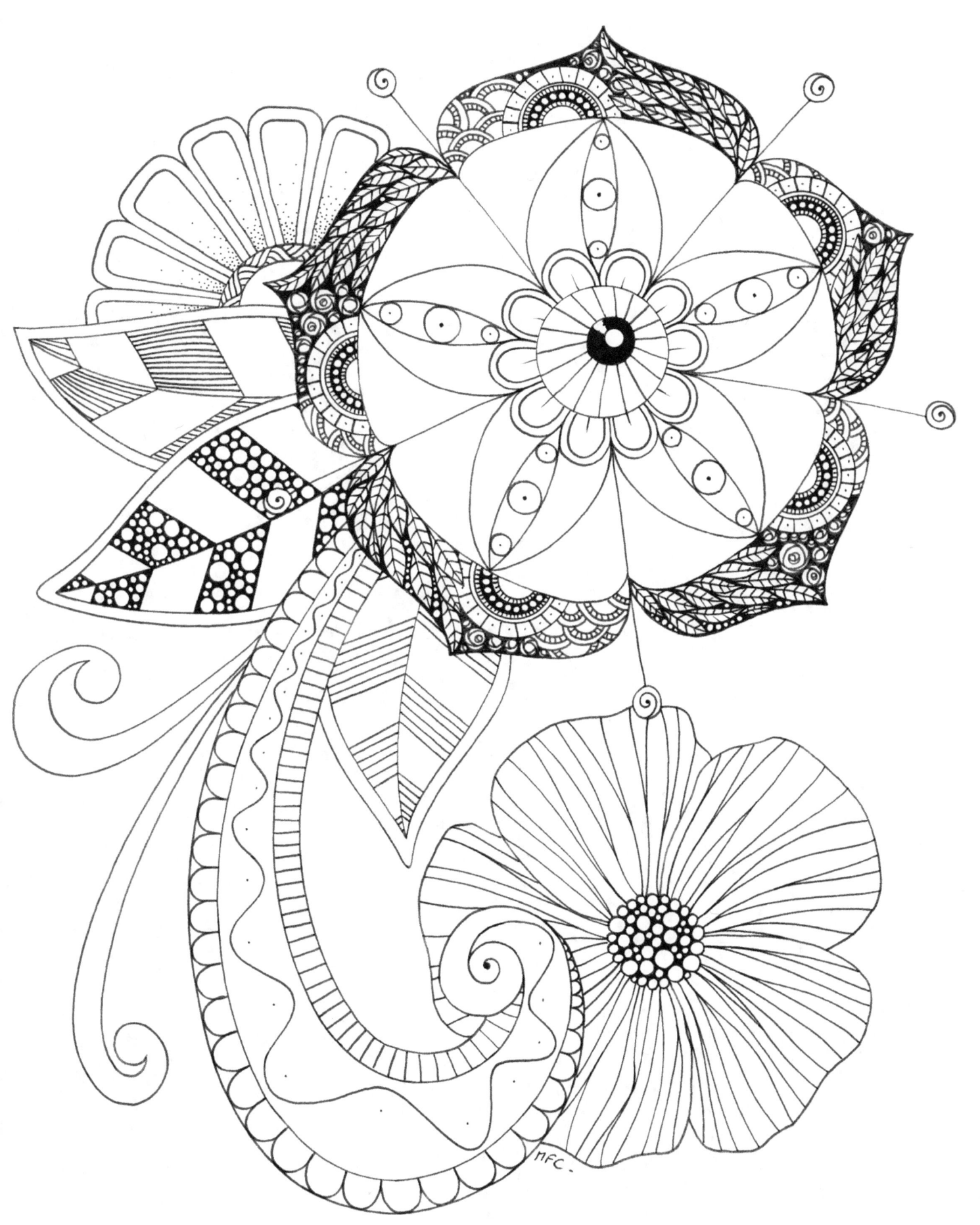

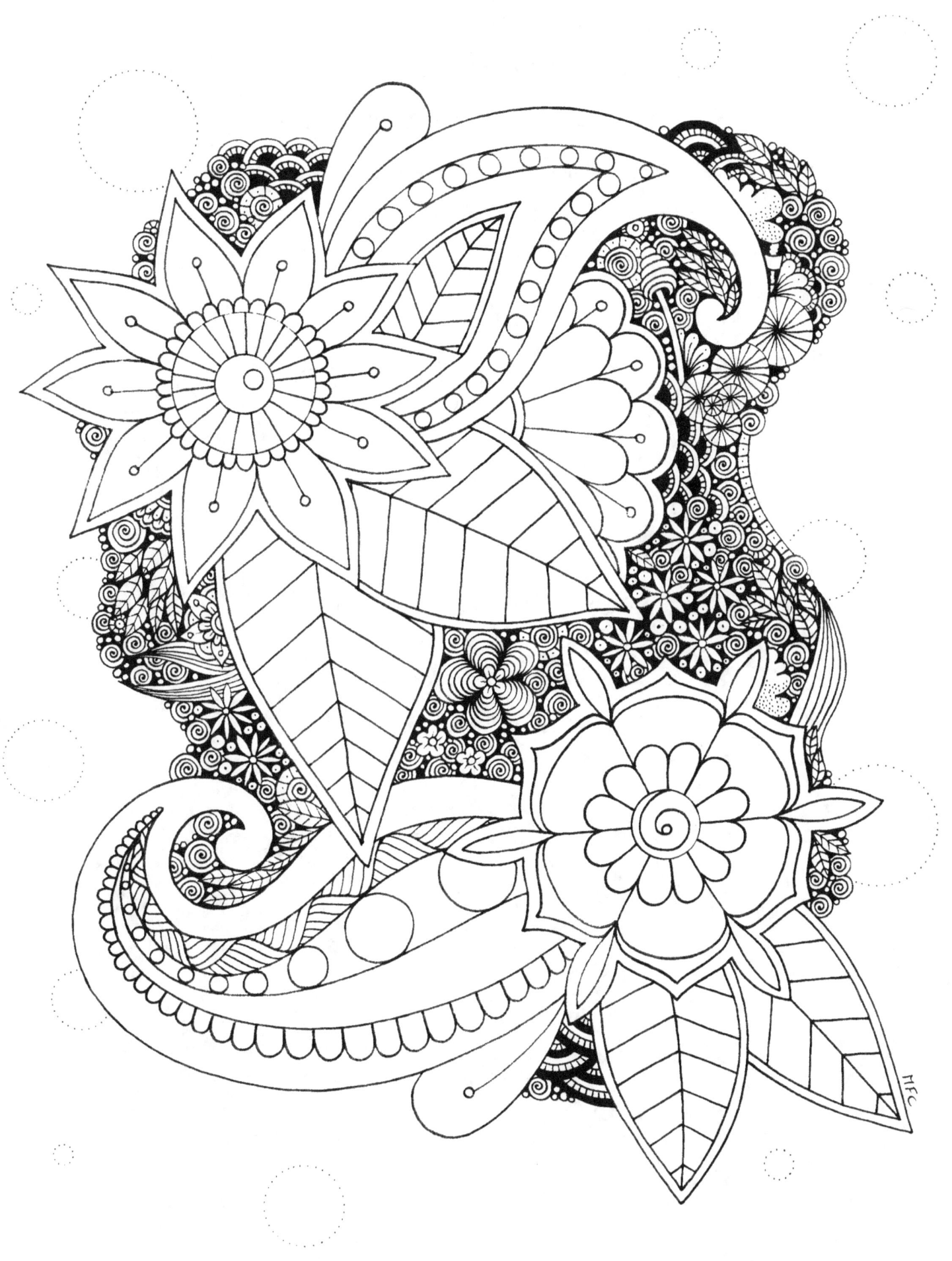

Contributing Artist
Audrey Sagh
Saskatoon, Saskatchewan Canada

Facebook : AMS-Artwork

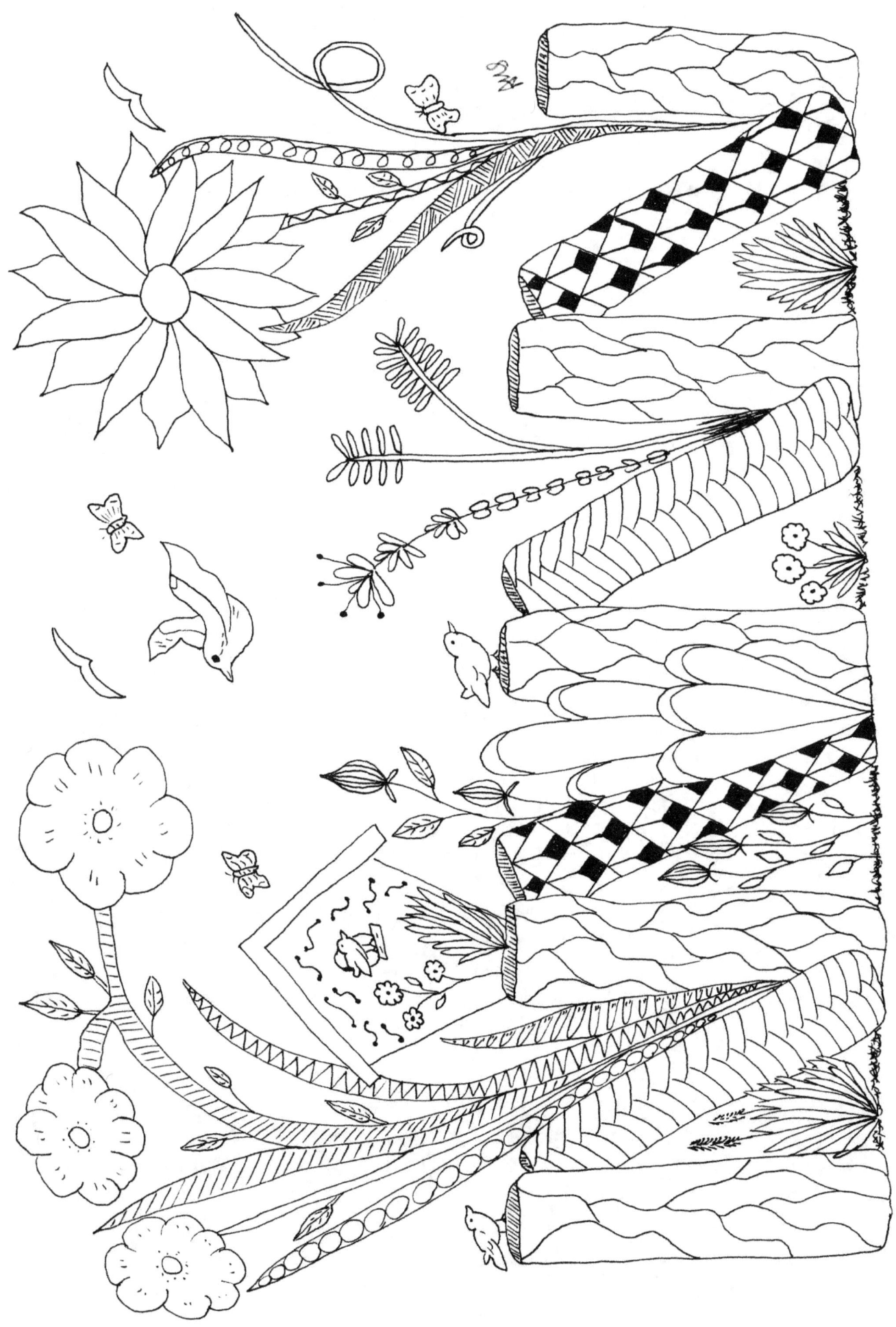

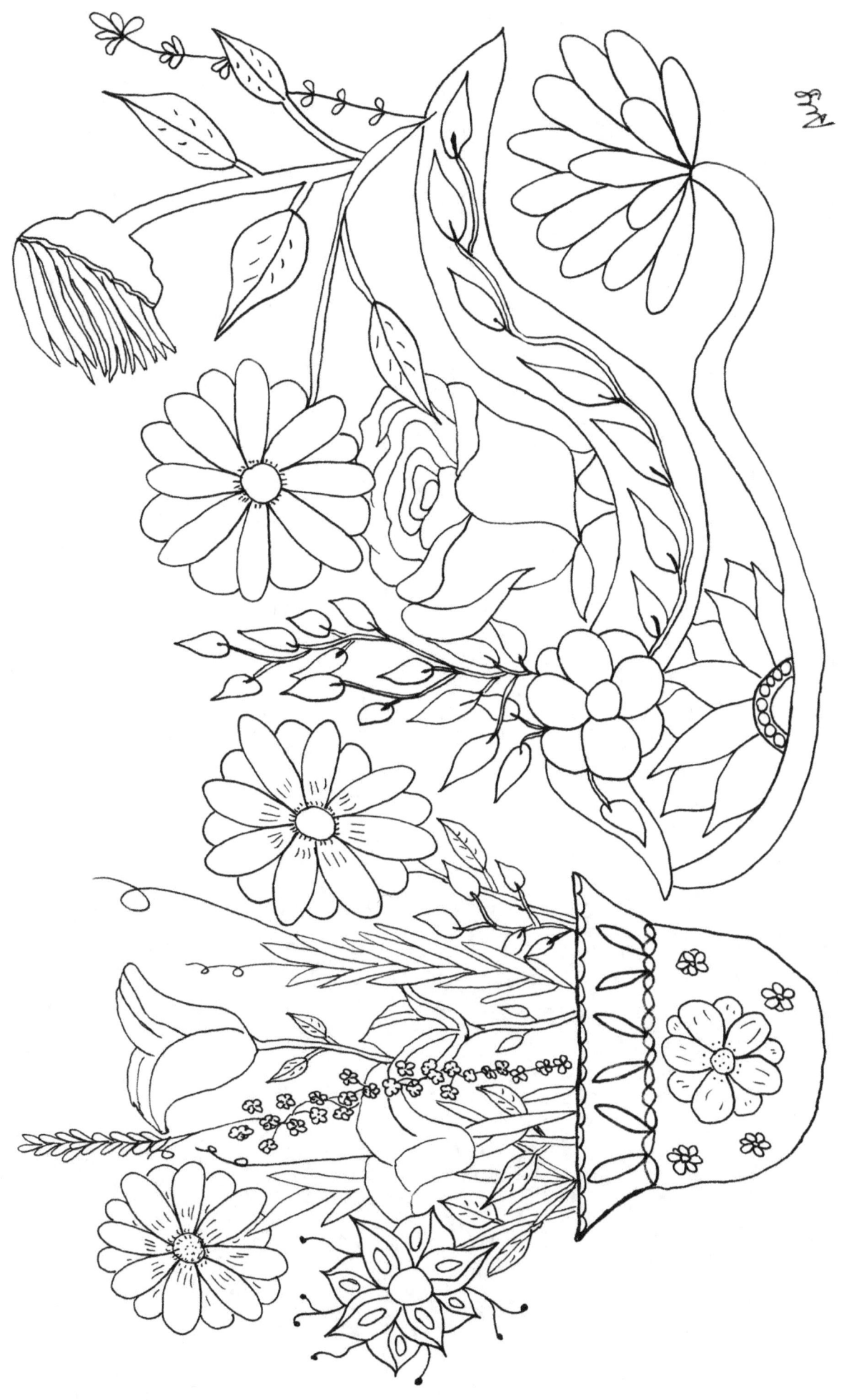

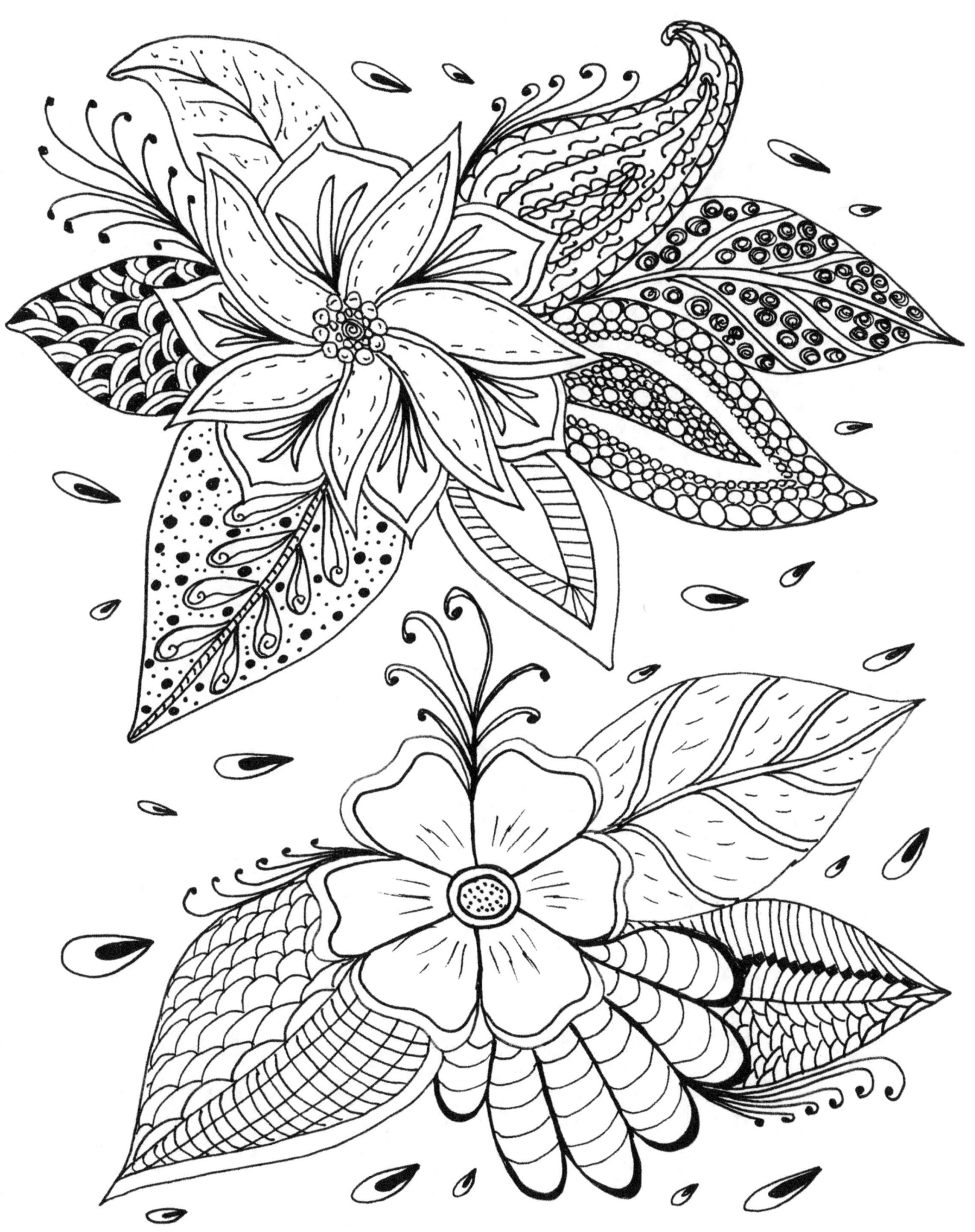

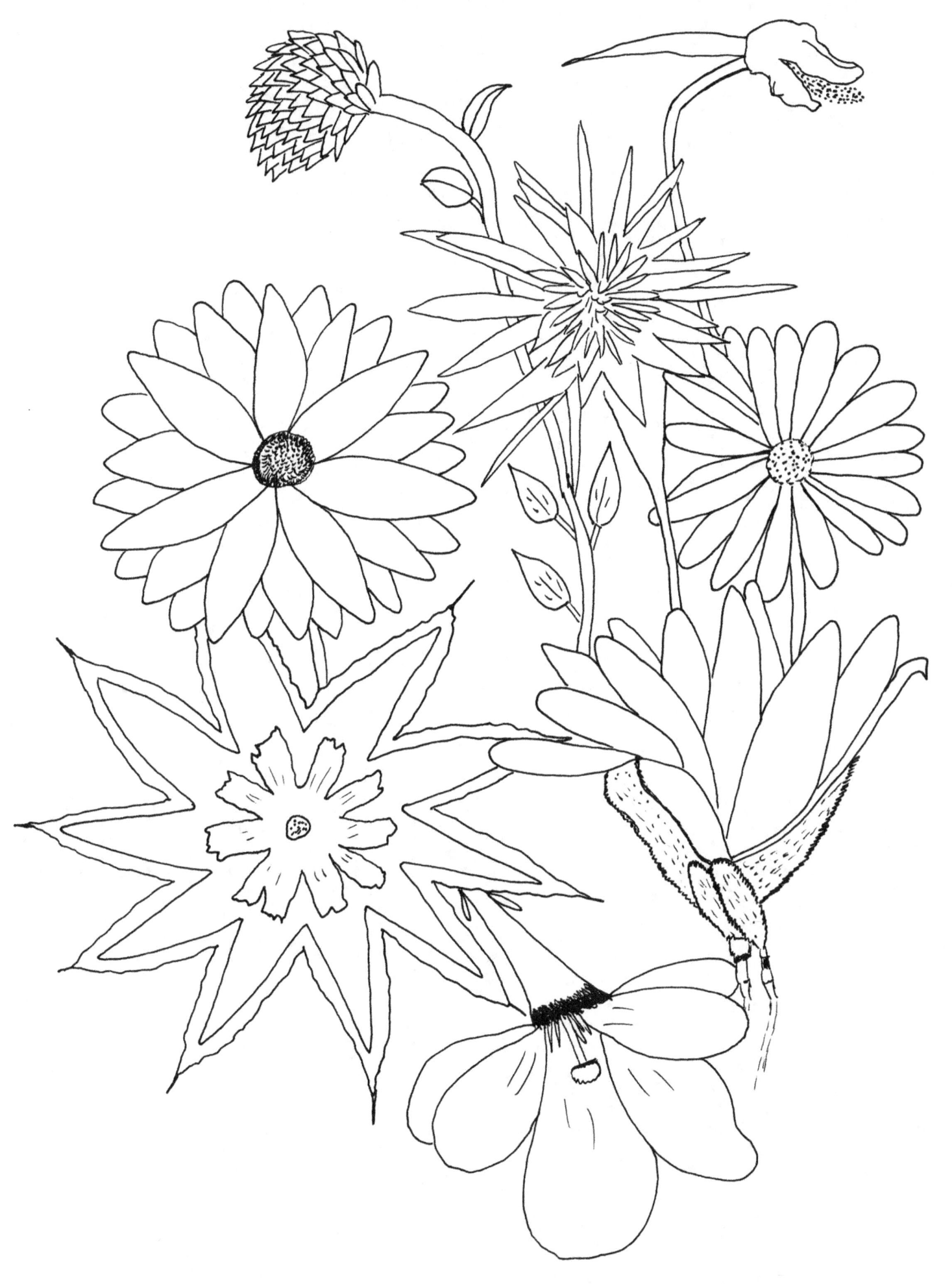

Contributing Artist
Nicole Whelan (Willow Hill Art)
WI, USA

Facebook : WillowHillArt
Etsy shop : WillowHillArt

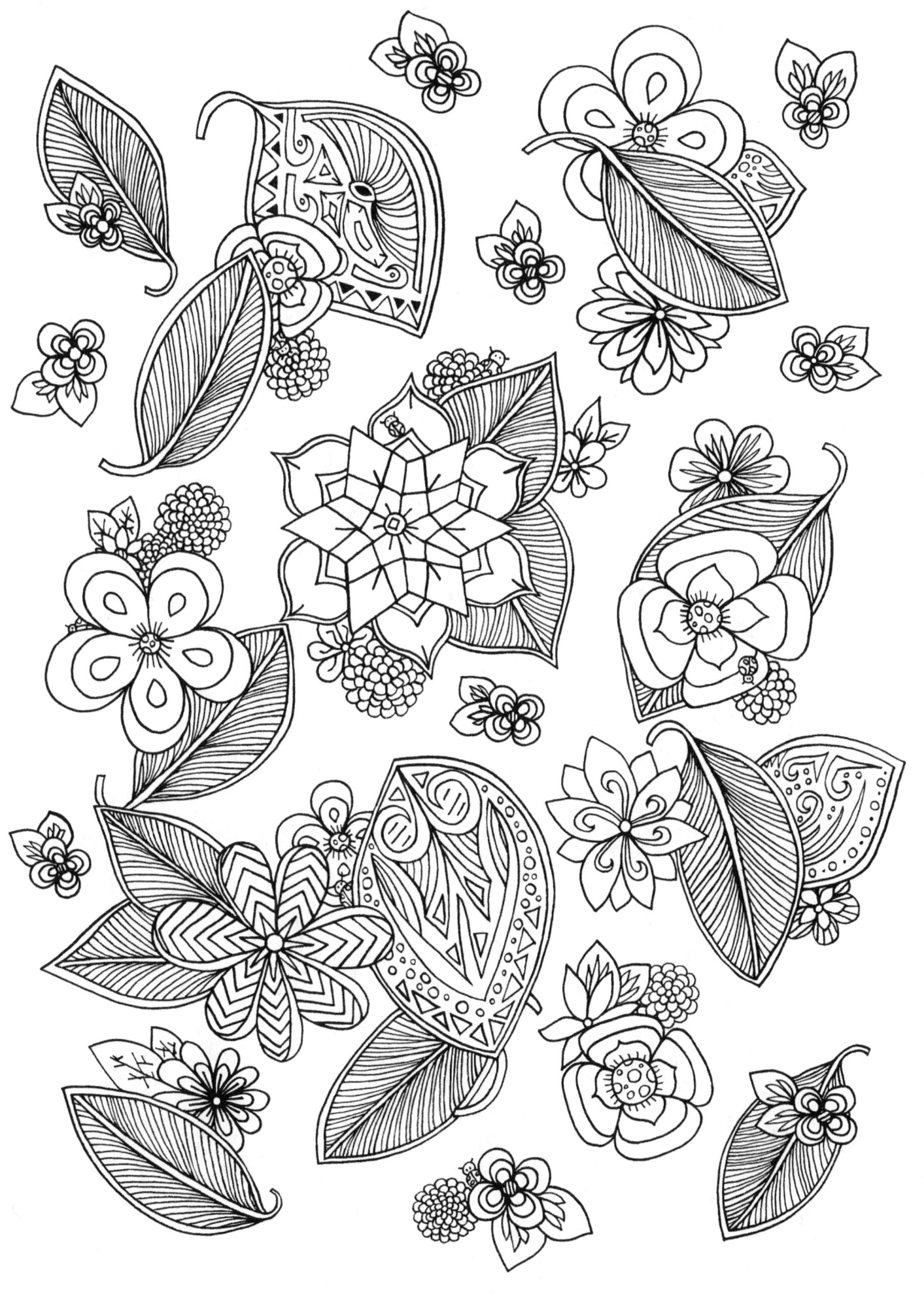

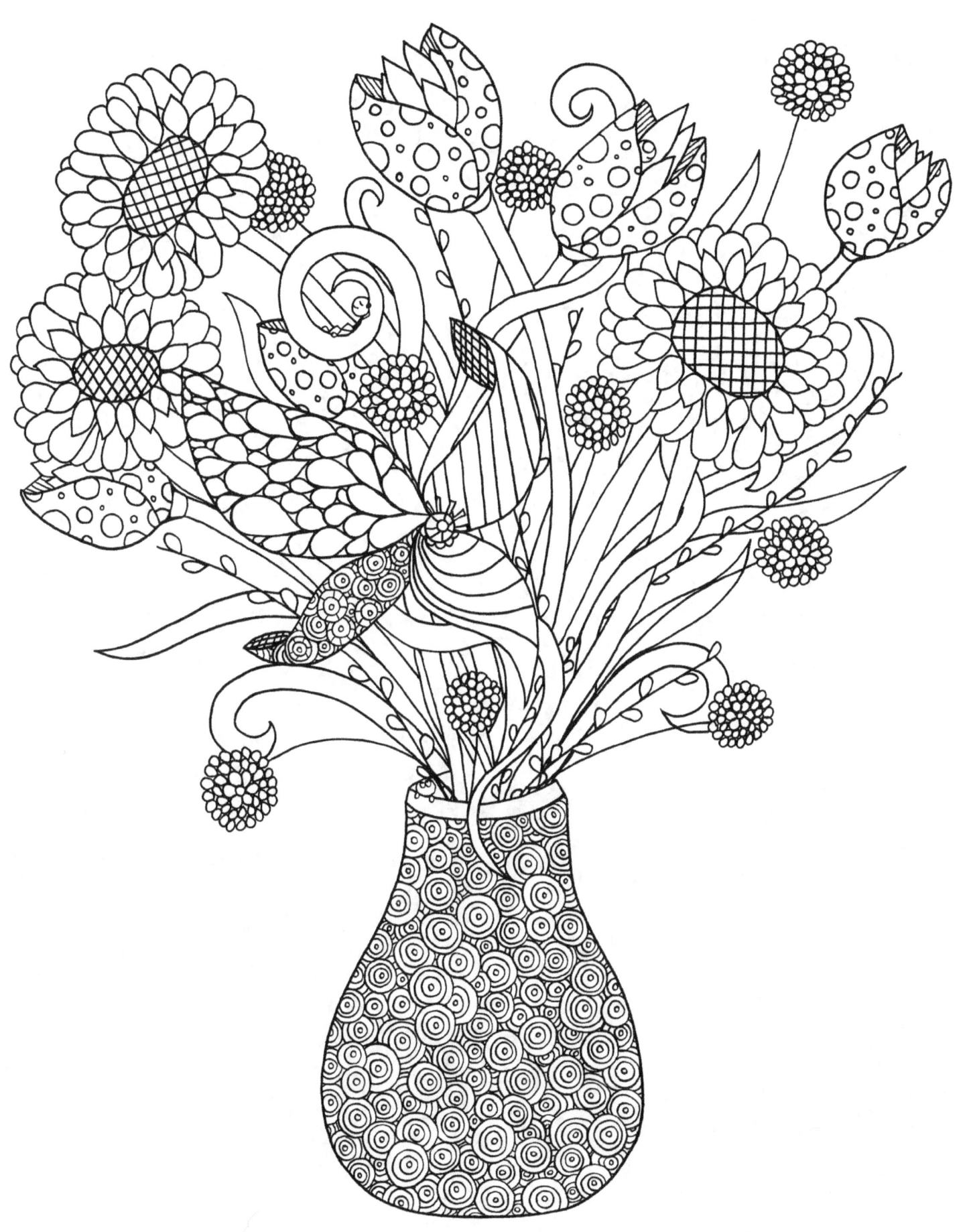

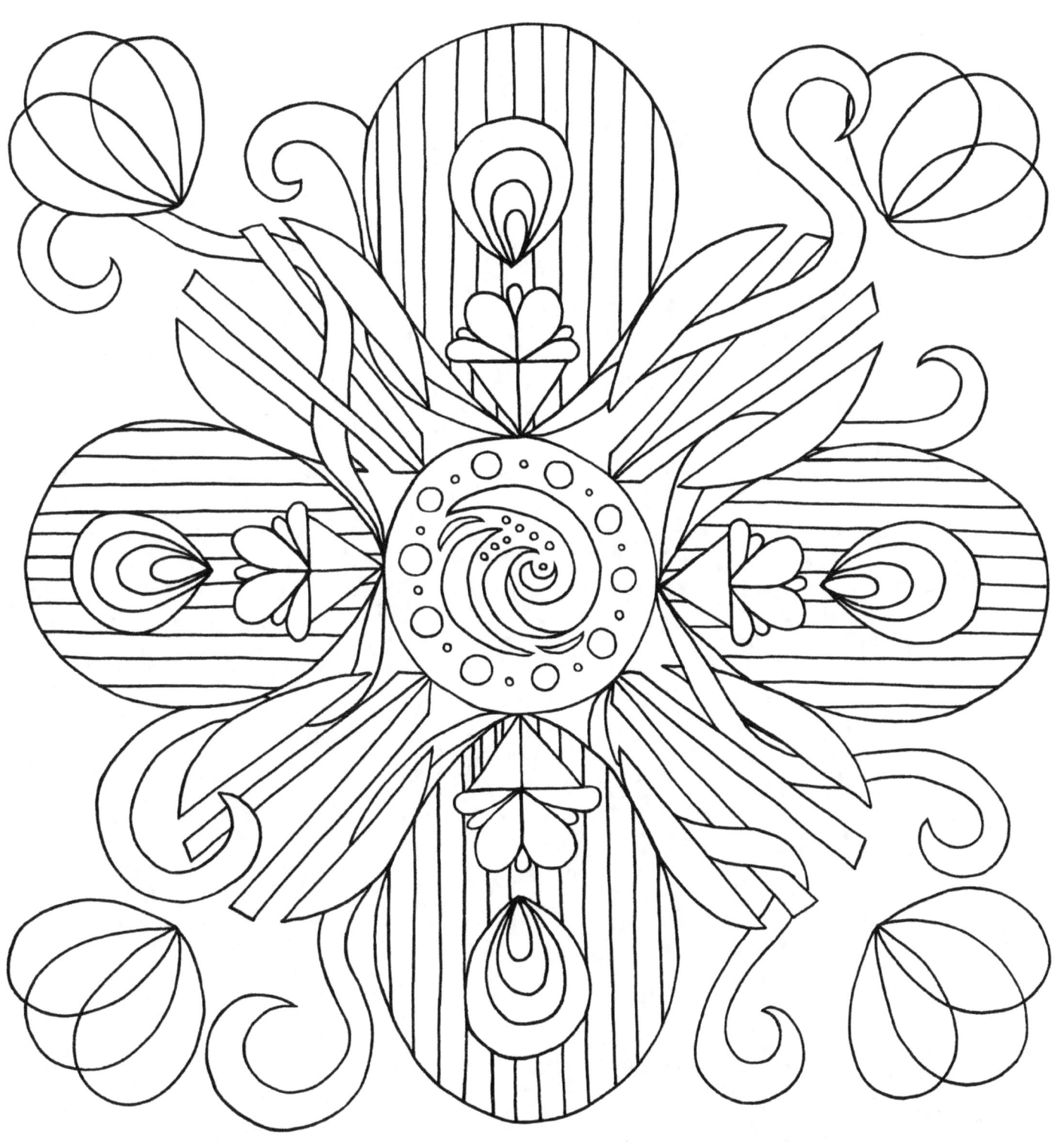

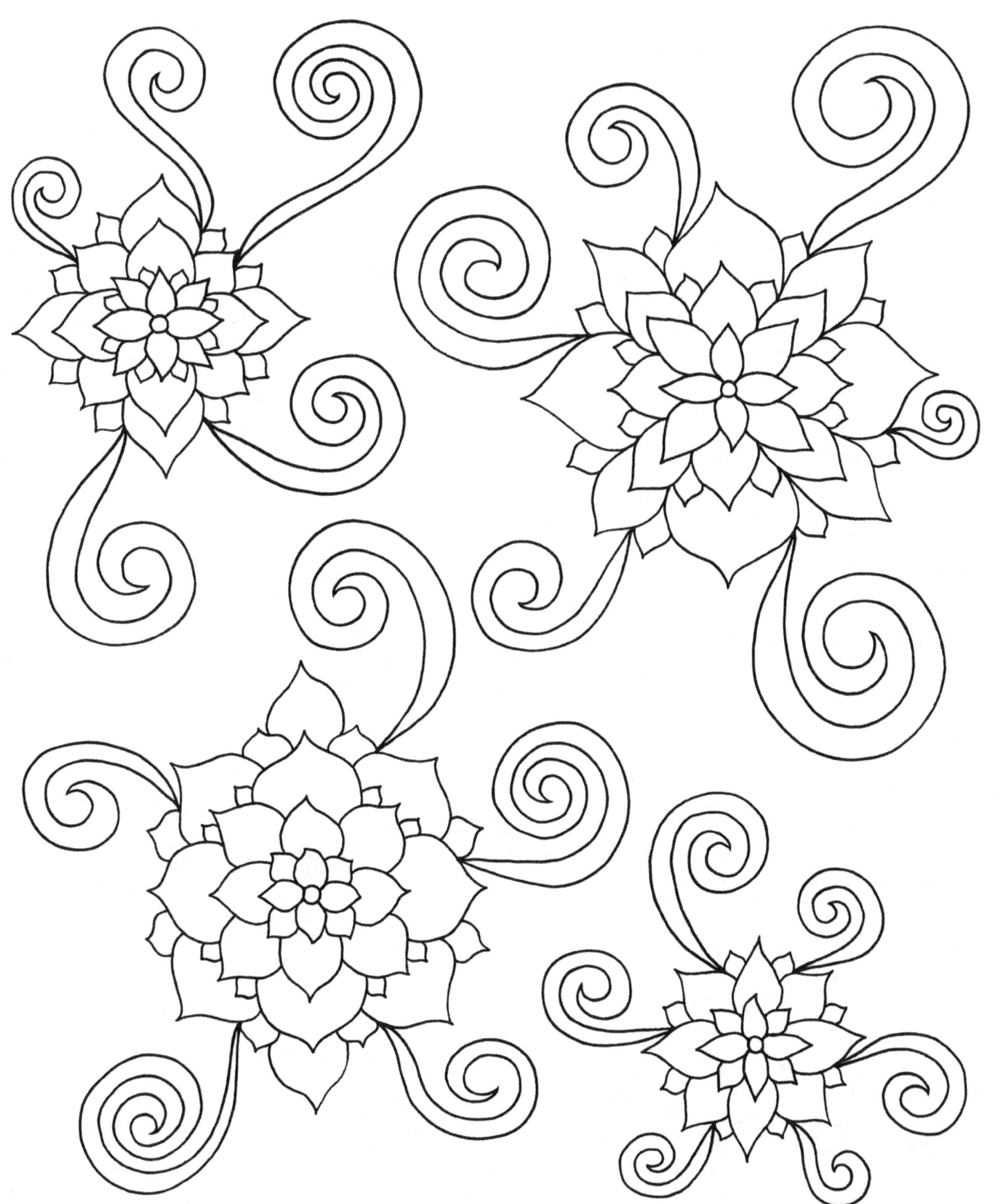

Drawn by Joseph Shivery & colored by Laurence Roucou	Drawn & colored by T.J.	Drawn & colored by Maud Feral Chauveau (MFC)
Drawn & colored by Iben Lykke Højholdt	Drawn by Jane Levi & colored by Mog Art	Drawn & colored by Nicole Whelan
Drawn & colored by Gloria Lenzen	Drawn & colored by Pica Wu	Drawn & colored by Marieke Raterman-Bos
Drawn & colored by Audrey Sagh	Drawn by Yaya & colored by M Lou Pencils	Drawn & colored by Lynne McGee
Drawn & colored by DomDomx	Drawn by Bev Choy & colored by Michelle Brotherton	Drawn & colored by Peggy Sue's Art Work

www.ingramcontent.com/pod-product-compliance
Lightning Source LLC
Chambersburg PA
CBHW082208220526
45470CB00010B/3088